The Mystery of the H. H. Holmes Collection

Alan E. Hunter

Irvington Historical Society Edition

The Mystery of the H. H. Holmes Collection
by Alan E. Hunter.
Indianapolis : NCSA Literatur, 2017.

ISBN: 978-1-880788-36-3

Edited by Steven J. Schmidt
and Paula Schmidt

Irvington Historical Society Edition

Published by
NCSA Literatur
401 East Michigan Street
Indianapolis, IN 46204
NCSALiteratur.com

Table of Contents

Foreword by Jeff Mudgett   1
Irvington and the Holmes Collection   3
Author's Preface   8

PART ONE: Holmes, the Man and his Crimes
The Devil's Backstory   15
The Devil Comes to the Circle City   21
Tracking Down the Devil   28

PART TWO: Artifacts
The Holmes Collection   37
The Michigan University items.   43
The Scalpels   54
Medical Ephemera.   60
Blood Relics   73
Written items.   76
Photographs   89

PART THREE: Suspects & the Holmes Curse
The Curse of H.H. Holmes.   113
Tracking down the Collection's Creator   123
Charles W. Miller   124
Detective David S. Richards   132
Pat Quinlan   137
Georgiana Yoke   148
Benjamin Pitezel   160
Emeline Cigrand   166
Frank P Geyer   172
Herman Webster Mudgett   177

PART FOUR: Epilogue
Hoosier Ties & Anomalies   183
Final Thoughts   187
Further Reading   189

Foreword

By
Jeff Mudgett, holding the University of Michigan
Graduation photo of his
Great-great-great grandfather, H.H. Holmes

From time to time, and as every real investigator hopes will happen with all their heart, an event occurs ratifying the very basis for an investigation itself. In that instant, evidence is located eliminating years of doubt and skepticism. Long questioned theories suddenly withstanding the light of day. Irvington's Alan E. Hunter and his wife Rhonda provided the team from ***American Ripper*** with just such a moment when they provided us the opportunity to inspect their boxes of H.H. Holmes mementos this past winter.

Filled to the brim with objects from the 19th Century, the boxes were a veritable time capsule to the killer's life in Indiana, Chicago, Michigan, and low and behold,

The Mystery of the H. H. Holmes Collection

London. English surgical tools, documents from the University of Michigan, the first real photographs of Holmes' assistants, and one small tintype which caught the attention of my Co-Host Amaryllis Fox. The image which forensic scientists would later determine had a very high probability of being that of Jack the Ripper's third victim, Elizabeth Stride.

All of us who were there will never forget that moment, especially when we are all constantly being reminded of its evidentiary importance by the hundreds of thousands of *American Ripper* fans who were provided the opportunity to share in its historical significance.

Jeff Mudgett
September 16, 2017

Irvington and the Mystery of the H. H. Holmes Collection

Irvington, known as the Classic Suburb, was the home of Butler University. The town was only twenty-four years old in the fall of 1894, and in addition to business and professional people making their homes in the suburb, it was also becoming a community of artists and writers. Located five miles east of the Indianapolis business district along the National Road, Irvington had been in the midst of a construction boom since the Citizens Street Railway had begun operating an electric trolley line between the city and town four years earlier and natural gas lines had been extended into the area.

One new resident was Dr. Thomas L. Thompson who had established a practice with Dr. John F. Barnhill in Moore's Block, 130 S. Central Avenue [Audubon Road], near the Irvington depot. In the summer of 1891, Dr. Thompson had a modest one and a half story gable front style house built on a large lot along Julian Avenue across from the Methodist Church for his family home. He later moved his family into a larger Irvington home and sold the property to George W. Lancaster for investment purposes.

The comings and goings of strangers on the trol-

The Mystery of the H. H. Holmes Collection

ley, or at the Irvington Panhandle Railroad station, or in delivery wagons was a common sight in this once bucolic community.

In the crisp, clear fall days as the leaves on the trees along the winding avenues of Irvington were changing from their dark green of summer to autumn's pallet of red, gold, orange, yellow, and bronze, Evil came to the little town in the form of Herman Webster Mudgett, a.k.a. America's first known serial killer, H. H. Holmes. On Friday, October fifth, a man using the name of A. D. Laws rented the Thompson/Lancaster cottage at 5825 Julian Avenue. He claimed the house was for his sister, Mrs. A. E. Cook. Over the next several days, the man was seen with a little ten-year old boy at the cottage and at a nearby drugstore. On Wednesday, October tenth, the man appeared at Pike's grocery, a few blocks from the cottage, on Washington St (the National Road). He had a boy's overcoat with him, and told the proprietor "a boy would call for it." The man was later identified as Holmes.

The following pages describe a collection of items attributed to Holmes that he left behind in Indiana. A consummate con artist, Holmes raised suspicions on a claim filed with the Fidelity Mutual Life Insurance Association in connection with the death of Benjamin Pitezel. The firm asked the Pinkerton National Detective Agency to track him down. A little over a month after leaving Irvington, Holmes was arrested for insurance fraud and jailed in Philadelphia. In a Philadelphia courtroom on June 2, 1895 Holmes pleaded guilty to a conspiracy charge, which carried a sentence of two years, and he was confined in the county prison. However, questions remained about the case, especially the whereabouts of

The Mystery of the H. H. Holmes Collection

Pitezel and his children. The district attorney's office asked veteran Philadelphia police detective and Pinkerton agent, Frank P. Geyer to investigate, and on the evening of June 26, 1895 he left the City of Brotherly Love in search of answers.

Geyer followed the trail left by Holmes around the Midwest and into Canada in search of the missing Pitezel children. In Toronto, the decomposing remains of thirteen-year old Alice Pitezel and fourteen-year old Nellie Pitezel were found buried in the basement of a house. The trail led to Indianapolis, and eventually to Irvington where the partially cremated remains of ten-year old Howard Pitezel were found. Further examination of a corpse found in Philadelphia concluded that it was the body of Benjamin F. Pitezel. Murder indictments naming H. H. Holmes and his various aliases were quickly issued by authorities in Indiana, Ontario, Canada, and Pennsylvania. Since he was already incarcerated in Philadelphia, Holmes would first stand trial in that city.

On September 23, 1895, Herman W. Mudgett, a.k.a. H. H. Holmes, was arraigned in a Philadelphia courtroom for the murder of Benjamin F. Pitezel. The trial commenced on October 28, 1895 and on November 2, 1895 the jury returned a verdict of guilty. "Holmes Must Hang", the newspaper headlines proclaimed. A few weeks before he was to be executed, the ***Philadelphia Inquirer*** published Holmes' written confession to twenty-seven murders. While these are the murders to which Holmes confessed, authorities believed there may have been scores of unknown others.

Inside the formidable walls of Moyamensing Pris-

The Mystery of the H. H. Holmes Collection

on, H. H. Holmes stood on the gallows and met his fate on May 7, 1896. But, the Evil that Holmes did in life did not end with his execution. Mysterious deaths of those connected with the Holmes case has given rise to the "Holmes Curse." The little Irvington cottage on Julian Av was not exempt; several of those living in the house after Holmes experienced tragedies in their lives.

The Mystery of the H. H. Holmes Collection details the compelling, eerie, and true story of America's first known serial killer and a few of the items, with ties to the Hoosier State and the quiet suburb of Irvington, attributed to the Evil One. I hope that you enjoy reading it as I did.

Steven R. Barnett
Marion County Historian
Executive Director, Irvington Historical Society

The Mystery of the H. H. Holmes Collection

Author's Preface

Irvington is a special place. Bounded by history, dusted by mythology, the face of Irvington is chiseled by fact and freckled by theory. Perhaps, no other community in Indianapolis can boast of a more colorful past than can Irvington. Here, that past collides with the present every day. Retrofitting, reimagining, and reinventing take place every day in this eastside community. The past comes alive through the imaginative updates of Irvingtonians who would rather rethink than rebuild. In Irvington, it seems that the more things change, the more they stay the same. And that is a good thing.

In a few short years, we will witness the 200th anniversary of the first European settlement in the Irvington area in 1821. The town, as we know it, can be traced back to it's inception as a planned development in 1870 and annexation by Indianapolis in 1903. Over that century and a half, the community has been home to the very best and brightest minds in Indianapolis as well as a temporary host to some of its worst.

For the past 15 years or more, I have led historic, haunted tours through Irvington. Although the bare bones

The Mystery of the H. H. Holmes Collection

of the stories have remained the same, the gist is ever changing. More facts surface, witness accounts evolve and new evidence is found. These tours examine the darker side of the community by discussing the mysterious events and people involved, both past and present. This book is based on a mystery born on one of those lantern-led tours some 13 years ago.

One of the stories featured on these tours tells the story of H. H. Holmes, America's first serial killer, and the the property where he murdered 10-year-old Howard Pitezel. As we walked towards the next stop, an elderly couple approached me. They said that they had gone on one of my Greenfield tours and came on this one to hear about the H.H. Holmes house. They asked if I would be interested in a group of items related to the Holmes crime. They explained that the collection belonged to a relative and that they had no use for the stuff and "just wanted it gone." I answered affirmatively and asked them to catch me at the end of the tour so that we could talk more about their collection.

The tour continued with several more stops and stories and as usual, at the end of the tour, guests lingered for pictures and to relate stories of their own or ask for more details about stories from the tour. Unfortunately, I lost track of the elderly couple. With no further details and not knowing either their name or what the collection contained, I considered it no more than two ships passing in the night.

The following Saturday, the night of the Irvington Halloween Festival, we did two tours. My wife, Rhonda, stayed behind at the registration table to greet guests and collect tickets for the second tour while I led the first

The Mystery of the H. H. Holmes Collection

group through the streets of old Irvington town. During the frenetic action of the second tour, the couple from the previous weekend approached Rhonda with a box containing the collection they had mentioned to me the week before. They handed the package off to Rhonda with the prophetic admonition, "This is for Al. He is expecting these."

Rhonda assumed that I knew who these elderly gift givers were. So in the rush of activity, she graciously accepted the items and told the couple that I should be back to speak with them at any moment. Rhonda assumed that the couple would stick around and talk with me when I returned, but they left.

We were never able to reconnect with them. We never found their names or the provenance of the collection. The only clues they left were the statements that they had attended one of my ghost tours in Greenfield and that the collection of objects had "belonged to a relative."

It is important to keep in mind that at this time, no one was really aware of H. H. Holmes. The Holmes mania that exists today was nowhere to be found back then. The package that they left with Rhonda consisted of an innocuous cardboard box containing some loose photo pages and a pair of old fashioned book safes. At first blush, it looked like a pair of large dictionaries, with a rounded faux binding designed to hide its true intention and the contents within.

During a break in the activity on that Halloween Festival night, Rhonda's curiosity drew her poke through the contents of one of the book safes, accidently ripping the flap off of one of the boxes in the process. She immediately regretted her decision upon viewing the macabre contents within. She decided it was too creepy and re-

The Mystery of the H. H. Holmes Collection

closed the boxes. The boxes were placed in the trunk of our car and, owing to the excitement of the evening, forgotten.

The next day I began to pour over the items in this collection. Aside from a few relics that are easily connected to H. H. Holmes, most of the items in the collection remain a mystery. Over the years, I continued to study and separate them as best I could.

After being contacted by the film company for the **American Ripper** series in late 2016, my interest in the macabre memorabilia was rekindled. I decided to donate the collection to the Irvington Historic Society for display at the Bona Thompson Memorial Center

In the Spring of 2017, Rhonda and I, accompanied by Tim Poynter, agreed to meet with a producer from the movie production company. First, we met with Steve Barnett, Don Flick and Paula Schmidt at the Bona Thompson center for a preliminary review. The boxes, which had pretty much been mothballed for a decade, were opened and the contents revealed. I think it can safely be said that all who were present that day were intrigued and amazed. It was decided shortly afterwards that the collection would go on display at the Bona for all to see.

Paula Schmidt coordinates the displays and collections at the Bona. We discussed the layout of the proposed display and both agreed that it should be presented as a mystery, sort of a "whodunnit" to determine where the collection came from and what is the most likely connection to H. H. Holmes. Paula's husband, Steven, approached me and suggested that I write a companion book for the collection. This is that book.

The Mystery of the H. H. Holmes Collection

    We will present the evidence in two parts. The first part will examine the man and his artifacts. The second part will examine the most likely suspects to whom the collection may have belonged. So now that you know the story, let us try and unravel the mystery.

Alan E. Hunter
August 2017

Part One

Holmes - The Man and His Crimes

The Mystery of the H. H. Holmes Collection

The Devil's Backstory

Herman Webster Mudgett, *aka* Dr. H. H. Holmes.

There is a spot on the eastern edge of Irvington whose place in infamy is as frightening in history as it is in reality. In this sleepy little corner of a quiet college town, is where, in October of 1894, America's first serial killer once trod the soil.

That man was named Herman Webster Mudgett. He is remembered today as H. H. Holmes. Some believe that he killed over 200 people. He admitted to killing 27, including one in Irvington.

The quaint Victorian cottage located at 5811 Julian Avenue looks much as it might have back in the Autumn of 1894. Its gingerbread accents and finely crafted exterior elements belie the events that caused it to slingshot into the "Gay Nineties" headlines of Middle America.

The Mystery of the H. H. Holmes Collection

To truly understand the possible significance of this collection of artifacts, one must first understand Dr. H. H. Holmes and what made him tick.

Herman Webster Mudgett was born in Gilmanton, New Hampshire on May 16, 1861, barely a month after the first shots of the Civil War were fired. Young Herman became obsessed with death and the anatomy of dead bodies at an early age by practicing on family pets and neighborhood strays. After graduating from secondary school, he headed west to enroll in the University of Michigan Medical School, where he graduated in 1884.

While at the University of Michigan, Herman honed his evil skills by stealing bodies from the medical school and turning the cadavers over to insurance companies to collect the payouts from falsified policies. As this scheme began to wear thin, Mudgett moved on and started on the path of crime that he is remembered for today. Not only was Holmes a mass murderer, he was also a swindler, forger, arsonist, thief, kidnapper, and a bigamist.

Mudgett, now known as Dr. Henry Howard Holmes, made his way to Chicago where he quickly muscled his way into a partnership in a widow's prosperous drug store. Not long after, Holmes took over the store entirely and the elderly woman mysteriously disappeared. He bought a large parcel of land across the street from the drugstore and began construction on a hotel that would eventually be known as the "Murder Castle".

Holmes built his Hotel to coincide with the opening of the 1893 Chicago World's Fair. During the fair, Chicago was visited by 27 million visitors--nearly one quarter of the country's population at the time. It was at this fair where America would be introduced to products

The Mystery of the H. H. Holmes Collection

and services that we take for granted today: electricity, moving pictures, automatic dishwashers, the Ferris wheel, Hershey bars, Shredded Wheat, Quaker Oats, Aunt Jemima Pancakes, Juicy Fruit gum, Cracker Jack, Pabst Blue Ribbon beer, the Pledge of Allegiance and the zipper. No wonder so many people visited Chicago in 1893. Holmes welcomed hundreds of fair visitors to his hotel. As many as 200 of them never checked out.

    The "Murder Castle" was located on the corner of South Wallace and South 63rd Street in an area known as Englewood; less than two miles away from the fair. The 100-room Victorian style hotel was a full city block long and three floors tall. The street level featured Holmes's relocated drugstore, a jewelry store and a few other retail shops. The top floor featured regular rooms for hotel guests, and a windowless middle floor Holmes used as his torture chamber. The hotel was a confusing maze of mismatched architectural elements; doors that opened to brick walls, stairways that went no place and oddly angled hall-

Holmes "Murder Castle"

The Mystery of the H. H. Holmes Collection

ways that allowed Holmes to confuse his guests as well as offering a places to spy on his prey unnoticed.

These second-floor rooms were soundproofed with asbestos, windows that couldn't be opened and doors that could only be locked from the outside. Rooms featured hidden gas valves and trapdoors in the closets that led to greased chutes below the floorboards. These devilish slides were used to slide bodies down to the basement, which contained vats of acid and a large furnace.

Holmes would prey on young, single women coming to Chicago, either for the fair or in hopes of finding work. Sometimes, he would go so far as to place advertisements in the papers looking for unattached women to employ. To say he was brazen would be an understatement.

If victims were fortunate, Holmes would simply turn on the gas and kill them while they slept. But if Holmes took a fancy to a particular young woman, he would turn on the gas just enough to knock her out, then brutalize his victim for days before sliding the corpse down the chute into the cellar.

One of the reasons we will never know how many people Holmes killed is because he had a very efficient way of disposing of the bodies. He would dump the bodies in large acid vats hidden in the basement, or use a homemade crematorium on the grounds. One of Holmes favorite disposal methods was to clean his victim's bodies down to their bones and sell the skeletons to the University of Chicago Medical School for $75 each, no questions asked, as was the practice at the time. Holmes operated in this fashion for nearly ten years before being discovered.

The Mystery of the H. H. Holmes Collection

Eventually, as the World's Fair came to an end, Holmes felt the pressure of decades long practice of dodging of bill collectors and missing person inquiries. It was becoming clear to Dr. H. H. Holmes that the jig was up in Chicago.

Holmes returned to his college era scheme, partnering with his ex-con handyman and alleged accomplice Benjamin Pitezel, to make some easy money. First, Holmes advised Pitezel to take a large insurance policy out on his own life, with Holmes as the sole beneficiary. Then Holmes promised to find a recently deceased cadaver as a substitute. He would cash in on the policy, and split the proceeds with the family. Next, Holmes advised Benjamin's wife to do the same for three of the Pitezel children: Alice, Nellie and Howard. He promised to keep the children safe by shuttling them around the Midwest and Canada until suitable replacement corpses could be found to perpetrate the same scheme.

Benjamin Pitezel, Holmes' handyman and alleged accomplice.

Eventually, Holmes killed Benjamin Pitezel and collected the proceeds of his policy as the beneficiary. The deadly doctor then told the unsuspecting "widow" that her husband had to lay low for a while as he left with the three Pitezel children to implement the second, third and fourth

The Mystery of the H. H. Holmes Collection

parts of his devilish scheme.

Holmes kept moving in a wide circle around the Midwest, visiting St. Louis, Cincinnati and Toronto, Canada with the children in tow. By now, Holmes's "Murder Castle" had caught fire, perhaps as the result of another insurance scheme. The fire was quickly extinguished by the Chicago firefighters who, while looking for flare-ups and hot spots in the wooden hotel, were horrified when they discovered the tools of Holmes's murderous deeds and remnants of human body parts spread around the building. The Chicago Pinkerton Agency was called in and soon Pinkerton Agent Frank Geyer was hot on Holmes's trail.

The Mystery of the H. H. Holmes Collection

The Devil Comes to the Circle City

When the devil came to Irvington in the fall of 1894, he brought along an innocent little boy, the 10-year-old Howard Pitezel.

Holmes arrived in Indianapolis on a Monday, the 1st day of October with three of the Pitezel children in tow. He checked into the English Opera House Hotel, later moving on to the Circle House Hotel on Governor's Circle (present day site of Monument Circle).

On Friday, October 5, Holmes arrived in Irvington, Indiana. Irvington was the first planned suburb of Indianapolis, located just five miles from the center of the city. Founded in 1870 by two prominent abolitionist lawyers, Sylvester Johnson and Jacob Julian, Irvington was laid out with the romantic winding street pattern that was so popular at the time and included a park, schools and the newly renamed, Butler University.

Howard Pitezel, aged 10

Holmes chose this taciturn seat of academia on

The Mystery of the H. H. Holmes Collection

Indianapolis' east side for very specific reasons; it was quiet, secluded and surely the last place one would expect a killer to hide. He stopped at the grocery store owned by Sam Shank on the northeast corner of Arlington and Washing- ton street with 10-year-old Howard Pitezel in tow. There he introduced himself as A. D. Laws, a doctor and a dentist seeking a modest house to rent for his sister, Mrs. A. E. Cook.

He was referred on to the real estate agent, J. C. Wands, where he rented the Ir- vington Cottage, locat- ed in the 5800 block of Julian Avenue on Ir- vington's east side. He paid one month's rent in advance and accepted the keys. The one-and-a -half story cottage was located at the spot where Julian and Maple (now Bolton) Avenues crossed. It was then the far eastern edge of Irvington, about five miles from the center of the capitol city. Holmes rented the property for a singular reason; to kill the 10-year-old boy.

The "Holme's Cottage" on the far east side of Irvington, IN

At 5 p.m. on Saturday, October 6, he called upon a local handyman named "Mr. Brown" to make some minor re- pairs to the property. According to his own confession, Holmes became enraged at the perceived indifference to the repair requests. Holmes said, "I became very angry with him (Mr. Brown) and my only wonder is that I did not entice him to the house and kill him also. This small circumstance aided in bringing the crime home to me when it was made known to the detectives and considered

The Mystery of the H. H. Holmes Collection

by them with many other complaints of my violent and ungovernable temper that had come to their knowledge." Irvingtonian Brown had no idea how lucky he was.

On Sunday October 7, 1894 Holmes visited the drug store near the Irvington railroad depot and "purchased the drugs I needed to kill the boy, and the following evening I again went to the same store and bought an additional supply, as I feared I had not obtained a sufficient quantity upon my first visit."

On Monday, Holmes went about securing furniture for the house. He did this late in the afternoon and "as I wished to stay at Irvington that night I hired a conveyance and carted the goods to the house myself, keeping the horse there until the next day. It was also upon the 8th, early in the forenoon, that I went to the repair shop for the long knives I had previously left there to be sharpened."

Advertising notebook from Peninsular Stoves.

On Wednesday, October 10, Howard was playing outside in the yard when the final pieces of the murderous puzzle fell into place as Howard's trunk and a large woodstove were delivered to the cottage. Howard was unaware that he, his father, his mother and his two sisters were embroiled in a life insurance scheme devised and controlled

The Mystery of the H. H. Holmes Collection

by "Uncle Howard". Nor did he know that he was worth $10,000 ($270,000 in today's money) to Dr. Holmes. Provided, of course, that Howard was dead. As Howard gazed at the shiny new stove, Holmes told the young boy to go inside and get in bed; but not before he administered what he believed to be a fatal dose of medicine. Sometime later, as Holmes entered Howard's bedroom, he found the boy unconscious but still breathing. With no medicine left and no time to spare, Holmes strangled the remaining life out of the helpless, and hopefully unaware, young boy. According to Holmes, "As soon as he ceased to breathe, I cut his body into pieces that would pass through the door of the stove and by the combined use of gas and corncobs proceeded to burn it with as little feeling as 'tho it had been some inanimate object." The next day, Holmes took the dead boy's coat and presented it to the Irvington grocer as a gift for his children. In an earlier confession to police, Holmes said, "Howard was strangled by myself and I dismembered and burned his body, then buried it in a house outside Indianapolis."

Holmes left Irvington almost immediately and returned to the Indianapolis Monument "Circle House" Hotel where he had stashed 14-year-old Alice and 13-year-old Nellie Pitezel. He left town the same day with both girls in tow. A few weeks later, Holmes would murder the girls in a Toronto hotel.

In August 1895, a full ten months after Howard's death, Detective Frank Geyer arrived in Indianapolis and took the trolley to Irvington to search for the boy. He had visited Indianapolis at least three times looking for any trace of Holmes or young Howard, but had never checked in Irvington.

It was last on Geyer's list because, just as Holmes

The Mystery of the H. H. Holmes Collection

Newspaper sketch of 13 year-old Nellie and 14 year-old Alice Pitezel

had surmised. Geyer arrived by streetcar at the rail depot in Irvington. He walked into the real estate office of Crouse and Brown, which was attached to the depot, and pulled out the well-worn photo of Holmes he'd been carrying from town-to-town and asked the agent seated behind the desk, "Have you seen this man?"

When he showed the photograph of Holmes to the land agent, the subject was promptly identified as Dr. A. E. Cook who had rented the Dr. Thompson's house for his sister.

Irvington marshal, Sam Smith accompanied Geyer to the property but Holmes was long gone. However, the "Peninsular Oak" wood burning stove was still on the property. The stove's shiny silver face was dotted with a series of diamond shaped vents, perched atop a set of claw shaped silver legs. Geyer wrote later that "it looked like an ominous metal hornet readying to pounce". It stood out because it was much too large for such a small space. This stove was designed to heat a far larger building, and was almost industrial sized in nature, so it did not belong here.

The Mystery of the H. H. Holmes Collection

Puzzled by the stove's presence, but anxious to get word to his superiors that he had finally found evidence of Holmes and Howard in this college town, the pair departed for the depot to telegraph news back to Chicago.

Along the way, Geyer encountered a pair of young men and decided to press his luck by asking if they had seen the man in his photograph. The pair answered "Yes" almost in unison. They explained how they were present when that "old stove" arrived and were paid handsomely to move it into the outbuilding for "that creepy old dentist." They remember asking, "Hey mister, why are you burning wood? Everyone's going to gas nowadays, nobody uses wood anymore." They remembered the doctor's reply, made as he leered menacingly at the little boy playing in the front yard, as, "I don't use gas because gas is harmful to children."

Detective Geyer then asked, "Do you remember that man's name?" The boys looked at each other and said, again in unison, "Yeah, Dr. Cook. His name was Dr. Cook." An eerily ominous moniker to be sure.

As the Pinkerton agent and the sheriff continued towards the depot, word began to leak out that there were "big doins'" going on out at Doc Thompson's place. Aware that the house was unoccupied, three local boys, George Brown, Oscar Kettenbach and Walter Jenney decided to conduct a search of their own. The trio sneaked into the outbuilding. Soon the boys were rooting through the stove's ashes where they found some teeth and part of a jaw bone. They immediately ran down the street to present their discovery to Dr. Thompson himself. The good doctor told the boys to run to the depot "fast as you can and fetch those detectives back out here."

The Mystery of the H. H. Holmes Collection

When the ashes inside the stove were eventually searched, Dr. Barnhill, a partner of Dr. Thompson, found pieces of charred bone from a femur and skull located in the makeshift crematorium. According to the official report, "Detective Geyer returned to the house and found teeth and a jaw, which were identified by Dr. John Quincy Byram, dentist. Also found at the bottom of the chimney was a large charred mass" described as, "a petrified deflated football." The mass was set aside where an inquisitive Indianapolis policeman decided to take a hammer and a chisel to it. Legend claims that it popped open with a hiss like a ripe tomato; it would turn out to be the stomach, liver, spleen, and intestines of 10-year-old Howard Pitezel.

As if further evidence was needed, the police found a toy top in the house and pieces of a broken trunk hidden underneath the back porch. When the items were shown to Howard's mother, she identified them as belonging to her son. Worse, it was revealed that the toy had been purchased at the 1893 Chicago World's Fair. The police soon discovered that Holmes had dug several holes around the property where he buried the ashes of the young boy a handful at a time in an attempt to make him disappear.

The death of Howard Pitezel was the first murder to take place in Irvington.

The Mystery of the H. H. Holmes Collection

Tracking Down the Devil

The hero of this saga was Pinkerton detective Frank P. Geyer. Many researchers claim that if not for Pinkerton detective Frank P. Geyer, H.H. Holmes may never have been apprehended and brought to justice for his crimes. It was Geyer who doggedly tracked Holmes around the Midwest searching for the three Pitezel children.

It was Geyer who doggedly tracked Holmes around the Midwest searching for the three Pitezel children.

In late August of 1895, almost a year after Holmes left Irvington, detective Geyer sent a letter to his supervisor, about his thus far futile search, "By Monday we will have searched every outlying town, except Irvington, and another day will conclude that. After Irvington, I scarcely know where we will go." On Tuesday morning August 27, Geyer took the Interurban trolley line to Irvington, then the home of Butler College, which he describes as "a most beautiful town, about

Detective Geyer.

The Mystery of the H. H. Holmes Collection

six miles from Indianapolis."

Geyer later described his visit to Irvington, "a short distance from where the (street) car stops, I noticed a sign of a real estate office, and in we went. Opening up a package of papers and photographs which I have carried, and which I had untied and tied over 1,000 times, until it had become soiled and ragged from wear, I asked a pleasant faced old gentleman who greeted us as we entered the office, if he knew of the house in his town, which had been rented for a short time in October 1894, by a man who said he wanted it for a widowed sister. I then handed him a photograph of H.H. Holmes. The old gentleman who proved to be Mr. Brown quietly listened, and then adjusting his glasses took a long look at the photograph."

"Yes, said he, I remember a man who rented a house under such circumstances in October of 1894, and this picture looks like him very much. I did not have the renting of the house, but I had the keys, and one-day last fall, this man came into my office and in a very abrupt way said, I want the keys for that house. I remember the man very well, because I did not like his manner, and I felt that he should have had more respect for my gray hairs." All the toil; all the weary days and weeks of travel, toil and travel in the hottest months of the year, alternating between faith and hope, and discouragement and despair, all were recompensed in that one moment, when I saw the veil about to lift, and realized that we were soon to learn where the poor little boy had gone with Holmes when he came."

Real estate agent Brown took the detective to Dr. Thompson's office nearby; Thompson was the owner of the home rented by Holmes. When Geyer showed Dr. Thompson a photo of Holmes, the doctor recognized the

The Mystery of the H. H. Holmes Collection

subject as the man who had rented the property. Dr. Thompson called for his hired hand, a local boy named Elvet Moorman, for further identification.

Elvet told Geyer, "Why that is the man who lived in our house, and who had the small boy with him." When Geyer showed Elvet a photo of Howard Pitezel, he confirmed the subject's identity as the child he had seen with the mysterious man.

Geyer described the property as, "a one and a half story cottage, standing some distance from Union Avenue, in the extreme eastern part of the town. Across the street is a Methodist Church and two hundred yards to the south are the Pennsylvania railroad tracks. The house stands in a secluded place, and there are no other houses in the immediate neighborhood. To the west is a small grove of young catalpa trees, and to the east is a large common. There are two roads leading to the street cars which run into Indianapolis."

"On entering the house, we searched the cellar first. I found it divided into two apartments, the rear having a cement floor and evidently intended for a washroom and the front having a clay floor, but hard as flint. It was quite evident that there had been no disturbance of the floor in the cellar, and we decided to make a search of the outside. To the right wing of the house is attached a small piazza, with open lattice work under the floor." said Geyer. It was under this checkerboard floor that Detective Geyer found his first clues that Holmes had been there. He found pieces of a broken trunk and a couple of rusty toys. The trunk would be identified by Howard's mother as belonging to the Pitezel family and the toys had been purchased at the 1893 Chicago World's Fair for the young

The Mystery of the H. H. Holmes Collection

boy.

Geyer then turned his attention to the barn behind the cottage, "In the barn, I found a large wood stove called 'The Peninsular Oak'...The stove was three and a half feet high, and about 22 inches in diameter-the top working on a pivot. On top I found what appeared to be blood stains."

Later, Elvet Moorman would recall helping a man, who was traveling under the name of Dr. A. E. Cook, move the large stove in the basement. While "the little boy stood by looking on," Elvet remembered asking the man why he was not using natural gas. Dr. Cook answered that, "he did not think gas was healthy for children." By now it was getting dark and in the words of Geyer, "Several hundred people had gathered about the house, seriously interfering with our operations, but all expressing great sympathy with us in our work...I decided to defer further search until the following day." Geyer returned to the city telegraph office to wire word of his discovery back to Chicago.

A reporter from the Indianapolis Evening News, contacted Geyer by telephone and informed him that Dr. Barnhill, a partner of Dr. Thompson, was on his way to meet him with "something of importance to communicate to me. The doctor arrived in a few moments and opened a small package containing several pieces of charred bone, which he declared were a portion of the femur and skull of an eight and twelve-year-old."

Dr. Barnhill explained that after Geyer had left and the Irvington boys concluded their search, the doctor and several members of the press arrived at the site of the macabre discovery.

The Mystery of the H. H. Holmes Collection

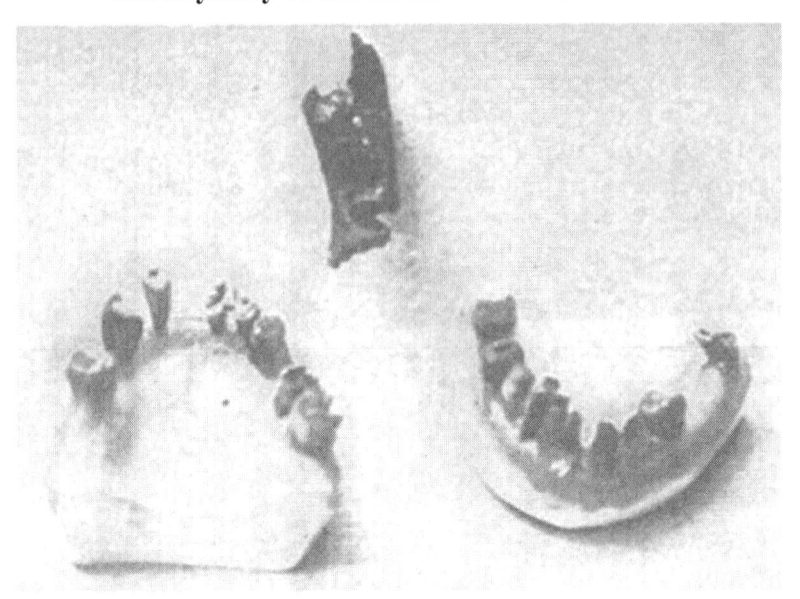

Photo of Howard Pitezel's teeth, found in the ashes of the stove.

Soon, Dr. Barnhill found "an old fly screen" and used it as a sieve to sift through the ashes and soot removed from the chimney. Barnhill said, "I passed it through the screen and found an almost complete set of teeth and a piece of the jaw...At the bottom of the chimney was found quite a large charred mass, which upon being cut, disclosed a portion of the stomach, liver and spleen, baked quite hard. The Pelvis was also found." Later these remains were identified belonging to 10-year-old Howard Pitezel. It would be determined that Howard Pitezel died on October 10, 1894 in Irvington.

A letter dated October 14, 1894, was found in the possession of Dr. Holmes while he awaited trial. The two-page letter from the childish hand of Alice Pitezel, Howard's older sister, was written just days after Howard was murdered by Holmes. The sadly sweet and innocent letter was addressed to their mother, but was never mailed. It contained a drawing of "Uncle Tom's Cabin" and an eerily

The Mystery of the H. H. Holmes Collection

prophetic message, "Howard is not with us now."

Another of Nellie's letters home (that Holmes never mailed) included descriptions of Indianapolis as seen from the eyes of a 14-year-old girl in 1894,

> "There is a monument right in front of the hotel where we are at and I should judge that it is about 3 times the hight [sic] of a five-story building. We ate dinner over to the Stribbins hotel where Alice stayed and they knew her to. We are not staying there we are at the English H(otel). We have a room right in front of a monument and I think it was A. Lincolns."

After his capture, detective Geyer closed the book on H. H. Holmes in Irvington, by remarking,

> "That night I enjoyed the best night's sleep I had had in two months. I was sure that my work was complete, and as I fell into an easy slumber, I thought that after all, the business of searching for the truth was not the meanest occupation of man. It is the manner in which it is searched for that sometimes makes it ignoble."

Holmes was put on trial for the murder of Benjamin Pitezel, found guilty and sentenced to death by hanging. On May 7, 1896, Holmes was hanged in the courtyard of Philadelphia's Moyamensing prison. The prison incidentally, was designed by Thomas U. Walter, the same man who later designed the House and Senate wings and the Dome of the United States Capitol.

The Mystery of the H. H. Holmes Collection

Until the moment of his death, Holmes remained calm and amiable, showing very few signs of fear, anxiety or depression. Perhaps because of his familiarity with grave robbing, he asked for his coffin to be buried deep and covered with cement to keep grave robbers from stealing his body.

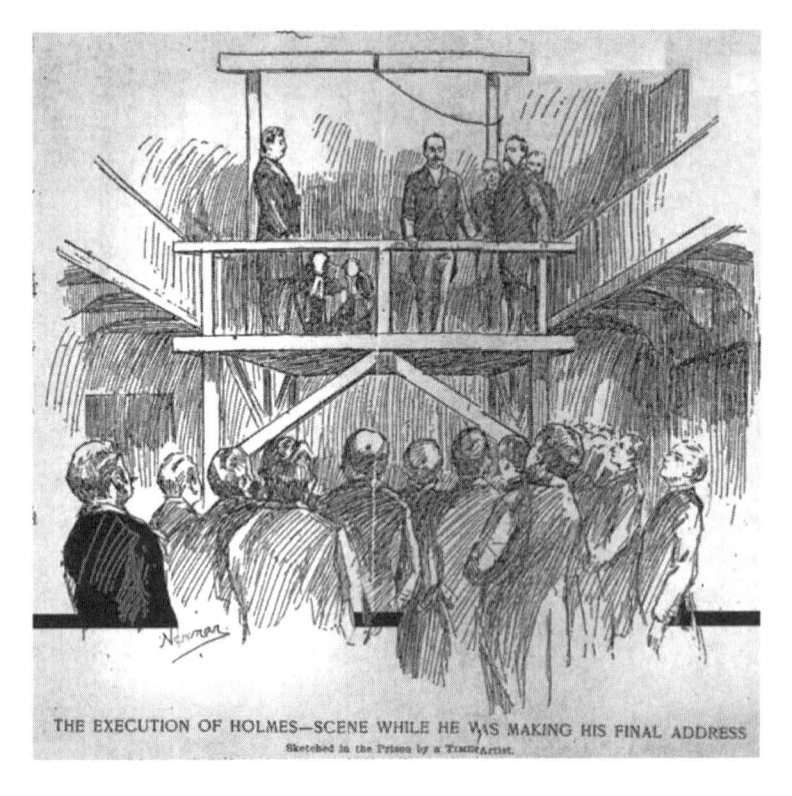

Newspaper artist's sketch of the execution of H. H. Holmes.

Part Two

The Artifacts

The Mystery of the H. H. Holmes Collection

The Holmes Collection

Researching Herman Webster Mudgett aka Dr. H. H. Holmes is a notoriously difficult task. First of all, Holmes was an inveterate liar. Like Ted Bundy, a century later, Holmes was not above offering tearful pleas and promises to reveal the names of more victims in order to delay his execution. Holmes's stories were inventive, offering a wide range of plausible explanations behind the disappearance of so many. According to Holmes, one person staged his own death in order to claim the insurance; another ran off to get married. Others he claimed killed each other, or were the victims of suicide, accidents, natural causes. Some, he claimed were still alive.

Second, in the age of yellow journalism, newspapers felt free to run stories filled with wild speculation on

Newspaper sketch of Dr. H.H. Holmes.

The Mystery of the H. H. Holmes Collection

the deadly doctor's deeds designed to sell more papers. The newspaper scholar, Frank Luther Mott, offered four characteristics for identifying yellow journalism: scare headlines in huge print, often of minor news; the lavish use of pictures, or imaginary drawings; the use of faked interviews, misleading headlines, pseudoscience, and a parade of false learning from so-called experts and a dramatic sympathy with the "underdog" against the system. All of which are evident in the coverage of Holmes misdeeds.

    Third, Holmes's neighbors were so eager to insert themselves into the narrative that they often fabricated facts to see their own names in the paper. And fourth, participants and officials involved were prone to the same type of exaggeration about their roles, often stopping just short of lying.

    Adding to this, is the mystery of the genesis of the collection itself. As previously explained, I was approached during the course of one of my Haunted Irvington tours some 13 years ago by an elderly couple interested in giving me a collection of Holmes relics which "belonged to a relative" and that they "just wanted it gone."

    We never learned who this couple was, or what the provenance of the collection was. The contents of the collection offer a wide variety of objects. While some appear to possess a direct line back to H. H. Holmes, the inclusion of other object's is unclear.

    It is important to keep in mind that this took place in 2002, before Eric Larsen's book, ***The Devil in the White City*** came out. At the time, few people were aware of H. H. Holmes or his crimes. The Holmes mania of today was non-existent at the time. With all this in mind,

The Mystery of the H. H. Holmes Collection

you can see how researching the contents of the Holmes Collection has proven to be confounding.

The package that the couple left with Rhonda was in an innocuous cardboard box containing a photo album, some loose photo pages and a pair of old fashioned book safes. The book shaped boxes are made of thin pieces of wood, covered with leather and marbled paper.

At first blush, they looked like a pair of large dictionaries, with a rounded faux binding designed to hide its true intention and the contents within.

These "book safes" contained a wide variety of object: over 100 photographs, three scalpels, handwritten notes, medical formulas and receipts, medicinal plants, a lock of human hair, bone artifacts, printed ephemera and assorted personal memorabilia.

"Book Safes" containing the Holmes Collection. Each box is 11½" tall by 9" deep and 3¼" thick. Front view, above and Rear view (open), below.

The items in the collection that are directly traceable to Holmes himself, include an autopsy photo, a personal stickpin and his

The Mystery of the H. H. Holmes Collection

graduation program, contained in an envelope with his name written at the top, perhaps penned there by Holmes himself.

One of the most intriguing aspects of determining the origin of this potential treasure trove of "murderabilia" is the fact that H. H. Holmes was a known collector. For reasons known only to him, Holmes saved items associated, or belonging to his victims. He was arrested in Boston, on November 17, 1894 (while in the company of his Hoosier wife, Georgiana Yoke), he was traveling under the name of Henry Mansfield Howard. When his possessions were searched, a tin box containing business papers and private memoranda were found. Among the papers were about a dozen letters from Alice and Nellie Pitezel, written to their mother and grandparents from Cincinnati, Indianapolis, and Detroit. These letters were never mailed. Apparently, Holmes kept them as souvenirs. A number of letters written by Mrs. Pitezel in Detroit and Toronto, were also found in the box. Holmes undoubtedly had many opportunities to dispose of this damning evidence, instead he hung on to them as mementos. These souvenirs would ultimately cost their collector his life.

Not only was H. H. Holmes, America's first serial killer, he also set the mold for all who followed. He was a documented collector of macabre souvenirs relating to his crimes. When FBI Special Agent John Douglas, perhaps the best-known criminal profiler of the past four decades, describes the psychological profiles of serial killer as souvenir collectors, he might as well have been describing Holmes. On his October 6, 2012 blog, *Manhunters*, Douglas said,

The Mystery of the H. H. Holmes Collection

"Killers like to take trophies and souvenirs from their victims. Keeping some memento — a lock of hair, jewelry, newspaper clips of the crime — helps prolong, even nourish, their fantasy of the crime. In my research, I've seen this happen again and again."

Douglas states that murderers retain mementos as a form of reliving the crime. "Between crimes, often while targeting future victims, they'll pull out their trophies and relive the crime over and over in their minds. Though they may say they committed the crime, they never really accept responsibility." He continued, "They'll never say, "Gee, I'm so sorry for what I've done here." The tears may well up in their eyes, but—and I've always said this— they're crying for themselves. They could care less about the victim. Sometimes they'll 'BS' you into thinking they believe it's all their fault, but they're only going along with the program so they can get out of jail."

Douglas continues, "When they finally commit a crime, it's like they have a sense of ownership. It's an accomplishment and they feel so good about what they've done that they have to keep it going...Many of us get trophies for our accomplishments. For killers, taking souvenirs extends the fantasy into that realm. It's like in the Wild West, where they used to cut notches in a gun. The whole thing seems like it's relived. It's fantasy, but it never ends. It doesn't even end when you incarcerate the killers." Or in the case of H. H. Holmes, when he was dangling from the end of a rope.

Thirteen years ago, when this collection was acquired, the research on Holmes was sketchy; scant at best. As more information has surfaced about Holmes and his crimes, it becomes easier to identify patterns and hypothe-

The Mystery of the H. H. Holmes Collection

size theories about the collection. In the following pages, I will address the Holmes archive collection piece-by-piece. Along the way, I will attempt to explore their individual relevance to Holmes, his crimes, his victims, his family, his associates or his investigators in an effort to help identify, understand and explain their existence.

    The rest, is up to you.

The Mystery of the H. H. Holmes Collection

The Michigan University Items

Undoubtedly the easiest place to begin our search would be by examining the items with a direct connection to Holmes. Although, as discussed in future chapters, there are a few items in the collection that could be traced to Holmes's New Hampshire birthplace, some relics can be related to Holmes's college days in Ann Arbor, Michigan.

Herman Webster Mudgett entered the University of Michigan's Department of Medicine and Surgery in 1882 and earned his degree in 1884. Throughout the 1880s, the University of Michigan was notorious as a hub for body snatchers, who sold fresh corpses to medical schools. Like medical colleges in Indiana, Ann Arbor tacitly supported grave-robbers and viewed them as a necessary evil. After all, students paid tuition and the medical school dissection rooms needed corpses for their students to practice on. School officials often turned a blind eye to cadavers stolen from midwestern cemeteries by these unsavory "resurrection men".

While all medical schools followed this practice, the University of Michigan seems to have been the worst offend- er. Newspaper reports of the University of Michi-

The Mystery of the H. H. Holmes Collection

gan's ill-gotten gains appeared in the papers again and again. When the City of Chicago cracked down on body snatchers, the grave robbers simply began shipping their Chicago corpses to Ann Arbor. Undoubtedly, young Herman Webster Mudgett viewed selling dead bodies as a way to defray the cost of his tuition. Besides, Mudgett had been fascinated with death since his childhood, possibly triggered by being stuck in a closet with a skeleton in a New England doctor's office.

Newspaper cartoon of Holmes dancing with a skeleton

Grave robbing fed both his fetish and his pocketbook at the same time. In 1896, around the time of his execution, former Michigan classmate John Madden, wrote to the ***Journal of the American Medical Association*** his recollection of Dr. H. H. Holmes:

> *"He seemed to take a good deal of pleasure in the uncanny things of the dissecting room. One afternoon's conversation with him I remember distinctly. He talked a great deal about what he had done in the dissecting room with what appeared to me at the time unnecessary gusto, and told me that the professor of anatomy was to permit him to take the body of an infant home with him for dissection during the spring vacation. I asked where he would find a place to carry on his work without offending his neighbors, and he replied with something to the effect that he "would find a place."*

The Mystery of the H. H. Holmes Collection

Photograph of an Autopsy class. 8" by 6", mounted on a 13½ by 10¾" mat. The man on the far left is believed to be Herman Webster Mudgett.

    The object in the collection that first caught my eye was mounted in a period photo album. It is perhaps the most gruesome single item found within the collection. It is an image of five men posed over another man who is very much deceased. The corpse is splayed out on a rough wood table resting upon a pair of sawhorses. One leg dangles off the side and the head of the dead man has been turned for one last look at the camera.

    It appears to be a classroom lab scene from the 1880s. The man in the center is older, distinguished looking and most likely the instructor. He is flanked on both sides by younger, college-aged men. Three of the men are wearing smocks or coveralls, but the young man on the far left of the table is unprotected and wears a bow tie, bowler hat and sleeveless vest. This man is posed with his hand

The Mystery of the H. H. Holmes Collection

resting casually upon the cadaver's leg and his medical instrument stabbed into the wood plank before him (See Insert). His other hand is held mysteriously behind his back. This young man is Herman Webster Mudgett.

Holmes authority and author, Judy Nickles, offers additional proof of this man's identity when she reveals a little-known fact about H.H. Holmes. "Experts have determined that Holmes had a bit of a 'lazy eye'", says Judy, "You can tell that the man in this photo suffers from the same condition."

Obviously, one interpretation of this photo is that it depicts a budding serial killer and con-man in his earliest epiphanic pose, eerily foreshadowing the dark deeds to come. As unseemly as this photo may be, skeletons, corpses and death were a common theme in the Gilded Age. Victorian Era photography abounds with images of the dead. After all, Victorian nurseries were plagued by typhoid, measles, diphtheria, scarlet fever, rubella--all of which could be fatal.

Other images can be found of skeletons riding bikes, playing cards or posed among the living as a demonstration of cheating death. So as creepy as this photo may seem to our modern sensibilities, it was a perfectly acceptable souvenir to the men portrayed within it. It most certainly was a prized possession of young H. H. Holmes.

The next item found in the Collection features a direct, irrefutable connection to the young H. H. Holmes. It is a bifold program for the "University of Michigan Fortieth Annual Commencement, Thursday, June 26, 1884." The front cover has evidence of being attached to a scrapbook with a long strip of glue residue along the left edge. The program features a finely detailed woodcut image of

The Mystery of the H. H. Holmes Collection

University of Michigan, 40th Annual Commencement Program, Cover. June 26, 1884. Printed by Argus Print. 5½" by 8½"

The Mystery of the H. H. Holmes Collection

Department of Medicine and Surgery.
DOCTOR OF MEDICINE.

Edwin X. Amoss,
Belle Evans Anderson,
Zachary Taylor Arnold,
James Anthony Bach,
Judson Henry Bennett,
Harry Ervin Blackstun,
Asa Prior Booth,
Ida Rebecca Brigham,
Benjamin Isaac Couian Buckland,
Almond Eugene Calkins,
Hugh Cary,
Calvin Survill Case,
Albert Eugene Coy,
Marion Craig,
Sara Craig,
Minnie A. G. Crawford,
George Willis Crosby,
Austin P. Culbertson,
Sidney Hollister Culver,
Henry Clay Doan,
Charles Willcox Dodd,
William Milan Edwards,
Ferdinand Thomas Field,
Frank Marion Foote,
John Willis Fowler,
Albert Theodore Getchell,
Frank Mortimer Gier,
Marcia Gilmore,
John Lincoln Gish,

John Fred Griese,
Clinton Clay Hall,
John William Handy,
John Kennedy Hanna,
Francis Albert Hargrave,
George Stephen Hatch,
George Albert Haynes,
Lucy May Heath,
Lydia Higgins,
Wilbert Arthur Hobbs,
Edward Hofma,
William Bailey Hunter,
Woods Hutchinson,
Thompson Linn Iddings,
William Warren Johnson,
John Kelly, Jr.,
James Asahel King,
Richard Willis Kitchen,
William Whiting Lathrop,
Robert Charles Leacock,
Laura L. Liebhardt,
Clyde Clark Lovin,
Stephen Ludlum,
Frederick George Lundy,
James Henry Lyons,
John Madden,
Frederick Williams Main,
James Wesley McGregor,

Andrew Barclay Mercer,
Emma Wilson Mooers,
Albert Irvin Moore,
Herman Webster Mudgett, ←
William George Muir,
Marie Thecle Orglert,
Adelbert Orton,
Daniel Edward Osborne,
Herman Ostrander,
Ridley C. Paine,
Onesime Frank Paré,
William Townsend Philips,
Charles William Piper,
John Powers,
Augusta Louise Rosenthal,
Relief B. Seeds,
Mary Smith,
Walter Erastus Spicer,
Newton Tibbetts,
Frank Adelbert Tinker,
Julia Tolman,
Orville Cram Trace,
William G. Wheeler Tupper,
Iris Jones Vaughan,
James Glidden Vining,
James Elsworth Walters,
Frank D. Whitacre,
William Halleck White. 85

Department of Law.
BACHELOR OF LAWS.

Willis John Abbot,
Leonard Alger,
John C. Donnelly,
Homer Clark Faucher,
Paul Hutchinson,

Albert Laurence Joyce,
Henry Saint Julian,
Henry Symes Mahon,
Allen Mitchell,
Charles Henry Mitchell,

William Richard Sawyers,
Edwin Thomas Smith,
James Franklin Van Voorhees,
John Hampden Yocil, 14

School of Pharmacy.
PHARMACEUTICAL CHEMIST.

Charles William Allmand,
Edward Blum,
William Henry Burke,
Eleazer E. Calkins,
Elvin Tuttle Case,
Charles Lewis Coffin,
John T. Conrad,
William Hamilton Cooper,
John Thomas Craig,
George Maurice Cushing,
William Edward Damon,
George Vernon Dawson,

Mattie Eaton,
Franklin Herbert Frazee,
Llewellen Hall Gardner,
Calvin Pomeroy Godfrey,
Charles Booth Harvey,
Wilmer Brown Hoge,
Arthur Gilliam Hopper,
Charles Hueber,
Charles Norton Lake,
George Pawling Leamon,
John Davidson Muir,
Theseus David Pease,

Charles Sperry Peyton,
Charles Riebe,
Adolph Aaron Schott,
Albert Christian Schumacher,
Channing Smith,
Herbert Waldemar Snow,
William Edward Stevenson,
William Issachar St. John,
Frederick Augustus Travis,
Albert Tenney Waggoner,
Robert M. Wetzel,
Edwin L. Wilhite,
Will C. Wyckoff, 37

Homoeopathic Medical College.
DOCTOR OF MEDICINE.

Frank Belville Adams,
Henry James Allen,
Elder Edward Austin,
George Blatchford,
Frank Ashbury Cameron,
Frederick Morris Gibson,

Louisa M. Hayes,
Rufus James Hyde,
Frank Arthur Johnson,
Charles Lindley Johnson,
J. Kate Laub,
Mary Louise Lines,
Charles Douglas Long,

Charles Orville Munns,
Walter Hulme Sawyer,
John Raymond Shank,
Louis Norton Tuttle,
William Irvine Wallace,
Rosella Cynthia Wilder, 19

College of Dental Surgery.
DOCTOR OF DENTAL SURGERY.

Francis Emory Battershell,

Franklin R. Carson,
Charles Phillip Weinrich,

Alvin Ellis Unger, 4

Total, 261

University of Michigan, 40th Annual Commencement Program, Page 4.
June 26, 1884. Printed by Argus Print. 5½" by 8½"

The Mystery of the H. H. Holmes Collection

an ornate, steepled building from the University of Michigan campus in Ann Arbor. Hansom cabs and horse and buggy rigs pass on the dirt street in the foreground.

The program details the order of exercises, music, prayer and an address by assistant Bishop Henry C. Potter of New York, followed by the conferring of degrees. Degrees were awarded for Civil Engineering, Science, Philosophy, Law, Dental Surgery, Homoeopathic arts, School of Pharmacy and Department of Medicine and Surgery.

Eighty-five students, both men and women, were awarded their Doctor of Medicine degrees. The names of the newly minted sawbones appear on the back cover in three columns. The fourth name from the top of the third column is listed as Herman Webster Mudgett.

Incidentally, Mudgett was not the only infamous student enrolled in that University of Michigan, Class of 1884. Hawley Harvey Crippen studied at the College of Homeopathy during the fall and winter of 1882-83 but did not graduate. Crippen became the first criminal to be caught with the aid of wireless communication when in 1910, police arrested him for murdering his wife. He was subsequently hanged in London.

Holmes classmate, Hawley

Although both men were enrolled in Michigan's Medical Department, the fields of surgery and homeopathy were very different departments. Based upon what we know of the two men, it seems unlikely. The two men's personalities were quite dissimilar. Mudgett was known on campus to be charming and outgoing; Crippen, shy and reserved. But these two Michigan classmates did share

The Mystery of the H. H. Holmes Collection

one thing in common — both were tried, convicted, and hanged for murder in grisly cases that made sensational headlines on both sides of the Atlantic.

The most romantically stylized item within this section is what appears to be the graduation stickpin of young Herman Webster Mudgett. The ½" wide by 3" long gold-plated stickpin has the letter "H" contained on the front of the square faced shield that is attached to the top of the stickpin itself. Although austere in appearance, it bridges the alphabetical gap between young Herman and his dastardly triple H alias yet unborn. Was this a gift from a family member, a friend or a doomed paramour? In this case, the letter of this relic screams H.H. Holmes.

The next item in this category may be the most tantalizing and could offer forensic proof to the Collec- tion's ownership. It is an unused manila envelope from the Zoological Laboratory of the University of Michigan. It has blank spaces to write the pertinent information about the envelope's contents onto the front. When the collection was discovered, the graduation program was found inside of this envelope. The signature reads: "H.W. Mudgett".

The envelope identifies the printer as George Wahr of Ann Arbor. Born in 1861, the same year as Mudgett, Wahr was a bookstore owner and publisher in Ann Arbor. The son of German's who emigrated to Michigan in 1835, he began clerking in a local bookstore at the age of 14, and eventually bought that store in 1882 (with aid of two other partners). Five years later, he bought out his partners and became sole owner. Wahr specialized in student supplies, books, and stationery, but he also had a lucrative

The Mystery of the H. H. Holmes Collection

publishing business which printed tracts on various subjects. All this points to the envelope dating to Holmes's time as a student at the university.

    The signature at top is large and flourished, but was it written by Mudgett himself, or by another party? In the 2006 book Sex, Lies and Handwriting, authors

Unused envelope from the University of Michigan Zoological Laboratory. 7½" by 10½"

The Mystery of the H. H. Holmes Collection

Michelle Dresbold and James Kwalwasser analyzed the signature of Mudgett.

"First notice the blotch on the top of the H and the puddle of ink on the M in Mudgett. Blotches, puddles, and muddy-looking writing show murky and unclear thinking. These dark spots are signs that he was obsessive, morbid fantasies and will indulge, uncontrollably, in his sensual and libidinal urges. It is interesting to note that Jack the Ripper also had muddied handwriting."

The analysis continues, "The fact that the blotch on the top of the 'H' resembles a dagger is no coincence. Weapon-shaped structures in handwriting are always a bad sign. They indicate that the writer has hostile impulses and will not hesitate to use violence. Weapon-shaped structures show an especially dangerous person when they are found in the personal pronoun "I" or in the signature. They also often indicate a killer's weapon of choice. Mudgett, a trained doctor, used his surgeon's scalpel to dissect the corpses of his victims."

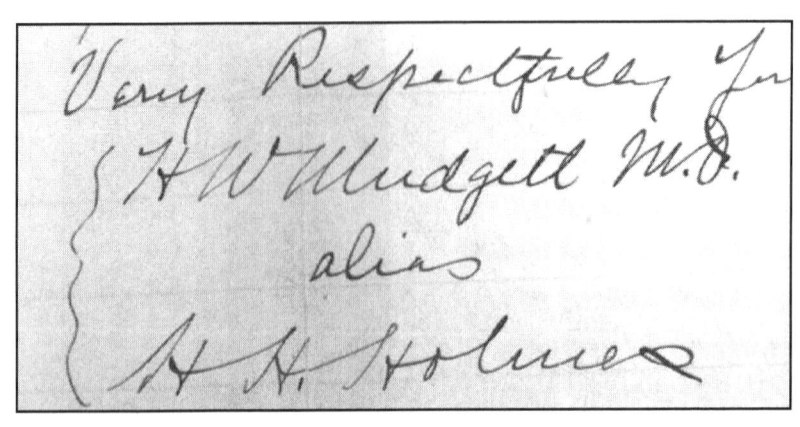

A confirmed example of Holmes' Signature.

The Mystery of the H. H. Holmes Collection

"Additionally, the flourished, curved double-cross of the "t's" in Mudgett might be viewed as a scar and the "d" resembles a mustache." The dagger points mentioned above can be found in the "H", "W", and "M" of the signature in this collection.

This signature in the Holmes Collection certainly resembles other known examples of Mudgett's handwriting, but there are also a few differences. Even if the handwriting on this envelope doesn't belong to Mudgett, it still indicated that it was once in his possession. Either way, the signature found here certainly represents contemporary evidence of the authenticity of the Holmes collection.

The Scalpels

Undoubtedly the most frightening relics found in the Holmes Collection are the scalpels or "bleeders". No other items within the bounds of this macabre group are able to convey the abject fear and sheer terror of H. H. Holmes better than these implements of pain. The frightening picture that these instruments represent, is particularly hard to ignore.

Strictly defined, a scalpel is a small light knife, usually held like a pen, and used in anatomical dissection and in surgical operations. Usually, the back of the blade is straight, or nearly so, the edge convex, and the point is very sharp. The handle is light and thin, long enough to pass beyond the knuckles when the knife is held in its usual position, and featuring a handle commonly made of wood, bone, ivory, steel or ebony depending on the era.

Early medical handbooks dating back to Holmes's era described the scalpel with typical Victorian Era prose:

"The manner in which a surgeon handles a scalpel is as important as its manufacture. The scalpel should not be grabbed as a hammer, a racquet, or a writing pen, but should be held as a violinist

The Mystery of the H. H. Holmes Collection

holds a bow. It should be held lightly by the tips of one's fingers and used with a graceful motion."

These journals further attempted to alleviate the negative aspect of the surgeon's tool by denoting:

"The knife handle appears to be dormant, a faceless object; but once its face is attached, it springs to life and becomes a scalpel. The surgeon has embraced this term, scalpel, for the surgical knife. "Knife" connotes danger. A knife is a weapon associated with mutilation and death, whereas a scalpel implies security, associated with healing. The knife can be used by anyone, but only a surgeon can wield a scalpel. The scalpel is an essential part of the surgeon's actions, and it is an instrument that demands respect. When properly used, the scalpel can perform miracles. Its misuse can cause catastrophes."

At first glance, one such scalpel in the Holmes Collection, contained in its black leather scabbard with a thin yet sturdy metal outer edge, looks as harmless as a

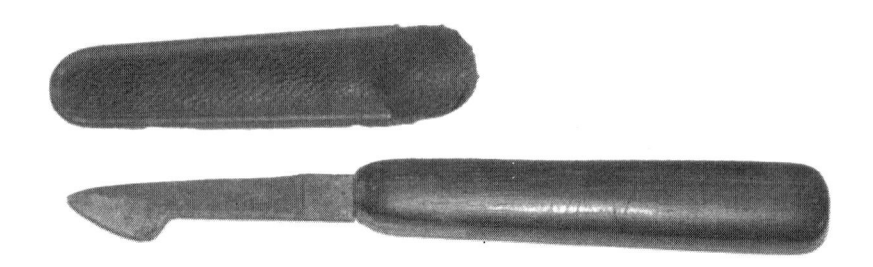

Scalpel with wooden handle and leather sheath. Marked with a fish logo. 5¼" long by ½" wide and ⅜" thick. Weight: .06 ounce.

The Mystery of the H. H. Holmes Collection

businessman's letter opener. It's thick rosewood handle displays the wear and rubbing consistent with generations of useful tutelage. But when the late-1800s era tool is removed from its leather holder, the truth is revealed.

The menacing looking surgical tool resembles a scaled-down version of a whaler's harpoon. The case hardened blade projects out from a rosewood handle to form an accentuated point with a razor sharp edge. The blade offers a ¾" inch cutting surface tapered for use to first penetrate, then neatly slice open the skin. The blade is marked with a fish stamped into an oval cartouche just above the scalpel's handle. The fish is undoubtedly the manufacturer's symbol from a long-ago blade maker whose identity we have not been able to identify.

The next item included in the collection is the most interesting of the lot. It measures 5½" long by ¾" tall by ¼" at its thickest point and weighs .06 ounces. Again, the handle is made of rosewood and the blade of hardened case steel. Like the scalpel in the sheath described previously, it has a tapered blade that resembles a whaler's harpoon. The blade is marked "R. Best Sheffield England" near the handle.

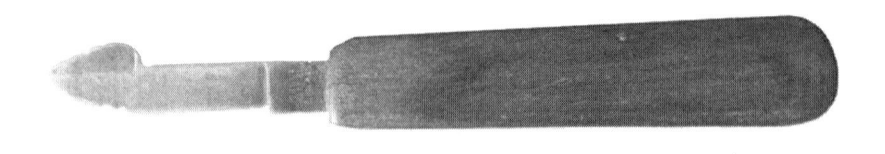

Top and side view of Scalpel with wooden handle. Made in Sheffield, England. 5½" long by ⅔" wide and ¼" thick. Weight: .05 ounce.

The Mystery of the H. H. Holmes Collection

What stands out most about this scalpel is its wear and patina. Dating from the late 1800s, it is easy to imagine that this blade has seen a lot of use over the years. When the instrument is taken in the hand, it glides into place like fingers into a glove. The wooden handle is tapered, or perhaps worn away, to a fine angle that accentuates the grip against the Proximal Phalanges between the thumb and index finger. The wear, weight and design of this particu- lar instrument form to the hand like a natural extension.

The blade tip has a razor-sharp edge on both sides, perfect for piercing, then slicing, into human bodies. Like the handle, the blade has seen heavy service with several nicks and dings caused undoubtedly by the instrument connecting with bone. Of the scalpels in the Holmes Collection, this is the one that calls out. This tool has its own vibe, its own mojo. It seems to throb, gently pulsate, even breathe on its own and silently scream H. H. Holmes.

The final instrument from the Holmes Collection is a curious looking device that looks more like a pocket knife than a medical device. The brass outer shell appears to be Medieval, and once the tool is unsheathed, the item looks downright primeval.

This instrument is a Phlebotome, known colloquially as a "Fleam", a tool most commonly used for bloodletting; the withdrawal of blood from a patient to cure or prevent illness and disease. Phlebotomy (from the Greek *phlebos*= vein and *tenmein* = to cut) the art of bloodletting, has been in common practice since ancient times. It flourished since the time of Hippocrates (5th century BCE) and is based on the principle of correcting the imbalance of bodily humors.

Three blades of this fleam are hidden inside the

The Mystery of the H. H. Holmes Collection

Brass and Steel Folding Fleam. Size: 3¼" long by 1⅛" tall by ¼" thick. Weight: 2 ounces. This folding Fleam has 3 double-edged blades which fold into a brass shield. The maker is C. Gregory of Sheffield, England.

brass hatchet shaped case. Each arm features one shark tooth shaped blade sized variously on the end. When fully extended, which was not the case for applied usage, the menacing looking item screams pain. One of the blades is marked "C. Gregory".

Gregory is listed as a Sheffield cutler in the mid to late 1800's. At the time, the best steel in the world was from the cutlery centers of Sheffield in England. The 1797 Robinson's Directory of Sheffield lists Gregory & Co. as "pen, pocket, and fruit knife manufacturers" located at 117 Pond Street.

While fleams were used on humans, they were also often used for veterinary purposes. These instruments, with their triangular-shaped blades, were designed to be placed over the vein and cut to allow the blood to flow

The Mystery of the H. H. Holmes Collection

freely. This would ideally result in a rapid penetration of the vein with little risk to the operator and minimal dissection of the subcutaneous tissues, the innermost layer of skin.

Once the desired blood was drained from the patient, the operator would place a pin through the edges of the incision. A figure-eight of horse tail hair or thread would then be placed over the pin to retain closure. By the latter half of the 19th century the perceived benefits of these bloodletting procedures were coming under fire and by 1900 fleams were considered obsolete. In America, fleams were in use in Antebellum Times through the Civil War and into the Victorian Era.

Does the inclusion of these macabre tools of the trade mean that the Collection once belonged to a surgeon?

The Mystery of the H. H. Holmes Collection

Medical Ephemera

There are items found within the Holmes Collection that can be traced back to a time before young Herman Webster Mudgett transformed into Dr. H. H. Holmes. Arguably these items could be found in any medical doctor's office or travel bag, but they take on a more sinister tint when viewed through the lens of America's first serial killer.

The Holmes Collection contains several handwritten artifacts. Although none of them are dated, the text was obviously written with a fountain or quill pen and the ink has become brown with age over succeeding generations. The text appears with the long fluid strokes made by a practiced hand in an age when handwriting was considered an artform. The documents contain many familiar, yet forgotten, terms and colloquialisms. Some of the words appear to have been written phonetically rather than with conventional spelling. These handwritten items were submitted for analysis in comparison with known examples from Herman Mudgett / H. H. Holmes. Although similarities were found, the results proved to be inconclusive.

While transcribing these documents for your pe-

The Mystery of the H. H. Holmes Collection

rusal, in instances where these word discrepancies appear, that word will be followed by the designation [*sic*] for clarification purposes. *Sic*, strictly defined, is a Latin adverb meaning "thus was it written". Traditionally it is inserted after a quoted word or passage to indicate an exact transcription as found in the source text that might otherwise be taken by the reader as an error in transcription.

The first document in the Holmes Collection is an ancient looking piece of blue colored paper titled: "Receipt for making ague pills." The formula reads as follows:

"Sulphate [sic] of quinine – – 40 grains. Gum myrrh – – 10 (grains). Liquorice [sic] – – 30 (grains). Triturate (grind or pulverize) well; moisten with a little water, and add just enough of the oil of safsafras [sic] to impart and agreeable oder [sic]; divide into forty pills; each pill then contains,

"Receipt for making ague pills"   7¾" by 5"   Written on unlined, blue paper.

The Mystery of the H. H. Holmes Collection

of quinine, one grain; of liqcuorice [sic], three fourths of a grain; of myrrh, one fourth of a grain. Dose, one pill; to be repeated every one or two hours, or longer to suit the case."

Strictly speaking, ague, the affliction for which this formula was designed to alleviate or cure, is described as a malarial fever whose symptoms include chills, shivering, fever, and sweating recurring at regular intervals. The term "ague" dates from the 14th century and was popularly used through to the end of the 19th century. It is a good example of how medical terminology changes over time. Not only are new terms introduced but old terms like "ague" decline in usage, and are dropped entirely. Today, ague would be called Malaria.

The ingredients listed within this formula sound ancient to our modern ears, but all were common terms for medicines back in the 1800s. Quinine was most commonly used to treat malaria, high fever and leg cramps. Myrrh gum, harvested from the sap of trees, was used for indigestion, ulcers, colds, cough, asthma, lung congestion, arthritis pain, and cancer. In traditional Chinese medicine, myrrh is said to have special efficacy on the heart, liver, and spleen meridians as well as "blood-moving" powers to purge away stagnant blood. The appearance of licorice in this prescription may seem out of place to present-day candy lovers. But to modern day *Twizzler* and *Good and Plenty* fans, it may come as a surprise that licorice has been used in medicine for thousands of years. Also known as "sweet root," licorice root contains a compound that is about 50 times sweeter than sugar. Licorice root has been used in both Eastern and Western medicine to treat a variety of illnesses ranging from the common cold to liver disease. It acts as a demulcent, a soothing or coating agent,

The Mystery of the H. H. Holmes Collection

and as an expectorant, meaning it helps get rid of phlegm. It is still used today for several conditions, although not all its uses are supported by scientific evidence.

The next receipt, or formula, may be the most intriguing based on its contents alone. It was written on a piece of ancient lined paper. This receipt was obviously made to be carried by the attending physician as it has the designation "Remedy for Colera [sic]," i.e. Cholera, on both front and back of the folded paper for easy storage and quick reference. The formula reads:

> "30 Grains of Sugar of lead. 30 Grains of Opium. 30 Grains of Assafeatry [sic]. 15 Grains of Cocaine Pepper. 15 Grains of Black Pepper. 4 Ounces of Brandy. Tak [sic] one teaspoonfull [sic] every two hours till Relieved. Shak [sic] the bottle well before taking it."

"Remedy for Colera" 7¼" by 5" Written on lined paper.

The Mystery of the H. H. Holmes Collection

    Ironically, the Sugar of Lead referred to in the above formula, is actually a salt with a sweet flavor. Known more accurately today as lead acetate, this deadly ingredient was used to make the medicine taste better. Before the Age of Enlightenment, the ancient Romans used the compound to sweeten wine and season food. Considering the physiological effects of lead poisoning, such as organ failure, infertility and dementia, we might find this ingredient frightening today, however, it was common in the late 1800s. Sugar of Lead can still be found in some everyday hair coloring products, whose boxes bear clear warning labels.

    This formula's use of cocaine may also be shocking to our modern sensibilities, but at the time it would have appeared quite normal. In 1885, the U.S. manufacturer Parke-Davis sold cocaine in various forms, including cigarettes, powder, and even an over-the-counter cocaine mixture that could be injected directly into the user's veins with the included needle. The company promised that its cocaine products would "supply the place of food, make the coward brave, the silent eloquent and render the sufferer insensitive to pain." By the late Victorian era, cocaine use had appeared as a literary device by Arthur Conan Doyle's fictional Sherlock Holmes, who offset the boredom he felt when he was not working on a case by using the drug.

    If the use of cocaine shocks today's readers, then the inclusion of opium in this prescription must elicit even more bewilderment. During the 18th century, opium was found to be a good remedy for many nervous disorders. And back then, a visit from the doctor usually meant one thing: pain. Doctors quickly discovered that, due to its sedative and tranquilizing properties, opium could help

The Mystery of the H. H. Holmes Collection

quiet the minds and lessen the anxiety of their patients.

The standard medical use of opium persisted well into the 19th century. Presidents Thomas Jefferson and William Henry Harrison, founding father Benjamin Franklin, first lady Mary Todd Lincoln, authors Charles Dickens, Lewis Carroll, Mary Shelley and her husband Percy are but a few famous opium users. During this time, users called opium "God's Own Medicine". An estimated 150,000 to 200,000 opiate addicts lived in the United States in the late 19th century. Between two- thirds to three-quarters of these addicts were women.

Another oddity is the inclusion of black pepper in this prescription. To most, this is a substance used to season food, not to make medicine, but in late 19th century black pepper was used to treat upset stomachs, bronchitis, and even cancer. At times, black pepper was sometimes applied directly to the skin for treating nerve pain (*neuralgia*) and the skin disease called scabies. However, in terms of this prescription, black pepper was most likely used as flavoring agent.

Finally, given the reputation of late 19th century medicine, the use of brandy may seem humorously appropriate. The inclusion of four ounces of brandy seems more appropriate for a shot glass than a prescription. Today, we typically view alcohol as an accompaniment to food, but back then medical professionals commonly fed alcohol to patients suffering harsh fevers. In some cases, alcohol could comprise as much as 40% of a patient's daily intake. No doubt, this additive resulted in the consumption of medicine by the patient long after the signs and symptoms for which it was prescribed had disappeared.

As for cholera itself, at the time this formula was

The Mystery of the H. H. Holmes Collection

written most physicians believed it was a locally produced illness, brought about by direct exposure to filth and decay. It was a common assumption that those who engaged in morally and physically intemperate behavior, or who had inferior cul- tural practices, were more likely to get cholera when ex- posed to these environmental conditions.

During the 19th century, cholera killed tens of millions of people with little distinction among victims; rich or poor, dirty or clean, famous or ordinary. Tchaikovsky, Beethoven, King Charles X of France, President James K. Polk and Patrick Kennedy (great-grandfather of John, Robert, and Teddy Kennedy) all died of cholera. It wasn't until the turn of the 20th century that scientists discovered that cholera was spread most commonly through food and water spread bacteria found on unclean hands, contaminated with fecal material.

The next handwritten document in the Holmes Collection is the largest in the lot. It is approximately 8" wide by 12½" long and, like the others listed above, the handwriting is ornate and flourished by vintage quill or fountain pen. The page contains three separate ingredient lists and preparation instructions, only one of which appears medical in origin. The other two recipes suited more for office use.

The first paragraph contains a compound for making "Black Ink". It reads:

"Black Ink. One pound logwood and one gallon of soft water, boil slightly or simmer in an iron vessel one hour; dissolve in a little hot water the grains bychromate of pot- ash. 12 grains prussiate of pot- ash and stir it into the liquid while over the fire; take it off, and strain it through a fine cloth."

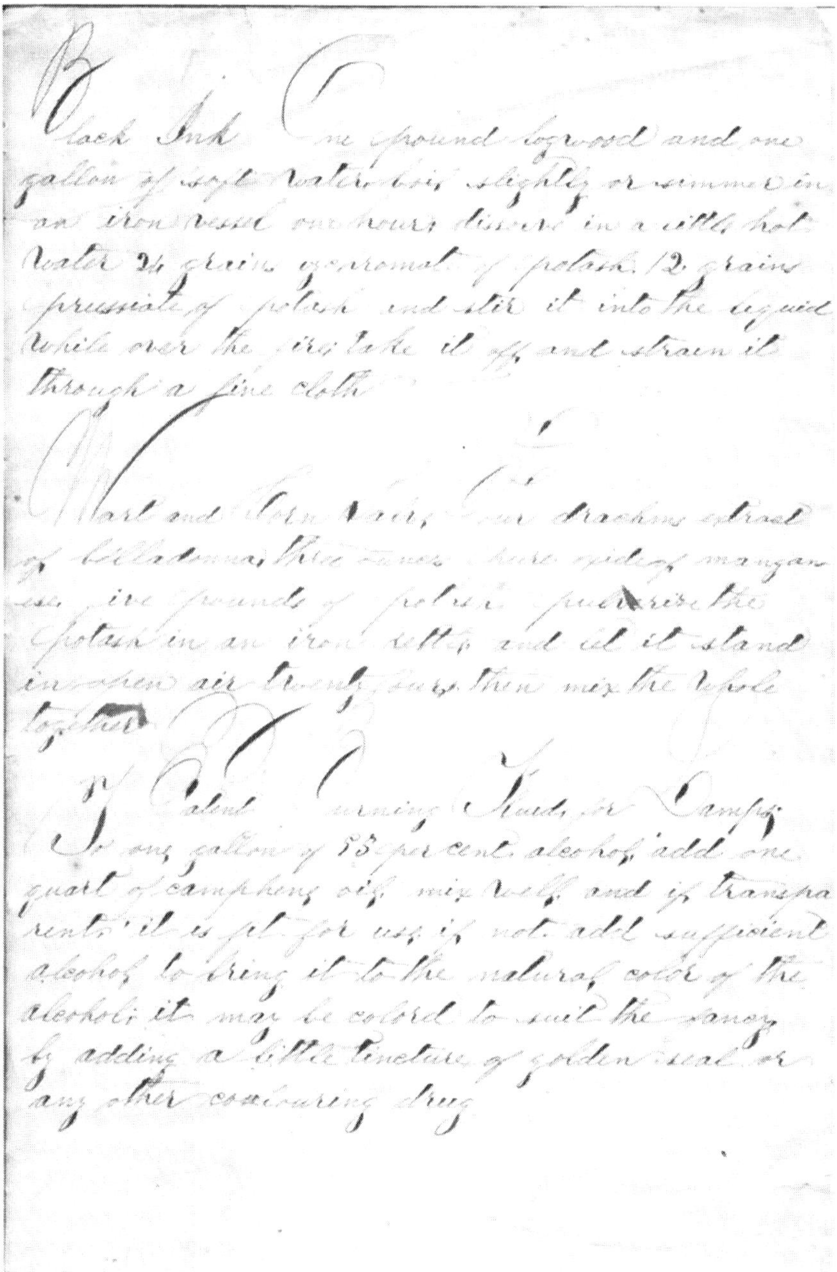

Black Ink One pound logwood and one gallon of soft water, boil slightly or simmer in an iron vessel one hour, dissolve in a little hot water 24 grains bichromate of potash, 12 grains prussiate of potash and stir it into the liquid while over the fire, take it off and strain it through a fine cloth

Wart and Corn Salve, One drachm extract of belladonna, three ounces black oxide of manganese, five pounds of potash, pulverize the potash in an iron kettle and let it stand in open air twenty four hours then mix the whole together

Patent Burning Fluid for Lamps

To one gallon of 85 per cent alcohol add one quart of camphene oil, mix well and if transparent it is fit for use, if not add sufficient alcohol to bring it to the natural color of the alcohol; it may be colored to suit the fancy by adding a little tincture of golden seal or any other colouring drug

"Black Ink", "Wart and Corn Salve", and "Patent Burning Fluid for Lamps.". 8" by 12½"

The Mystery of the H. H. Holmes Collection

The ingredients for this recipe are natural, wood-based materials easily found in nature.

The second paragraph contains a compound for making wart and corn removal salve. It reads:

"*Wart and Corn Salve. For [sic] drachms extract of belladonna, three ounces pure oxide of manganese, five pounds of potash.*

Pulverize the potash in an iron kettle, and let it stand in open air twenty hours then mix the whole together."

A drachm is equal to 60 grains or ⅛ of an ounce. Manganese is a derivative of metal not commonly found independently within nature.

The third paragraph contains a compound for making what appears to be fuel for oil lamps in the age before electricity. It reads:

"*Patent Burning Fluid for Lamps. To one gallon of 95 per cent alcohol, add one quart of camphene oil, mix well, and if transparent it is fit for use, if not, add sufficient alcohol to bring it to the natural color of the alcohol; it may be colord [sic] to suit the fancy by adding a little tincture of goldenseal or any other colouring [sic] drug.*"

This compound's ingredients, although volatile, were common in most homes, or found in any doctor's office or black bag during the Victorian Era.

For example, Camphene oil was used in perfumes and as a food additive for flavor. Alcohol, although highly flammable, is still used today as a common ingredient in

The Mystery of the H. H. Holmes Collection

antiseptics, disinfectants and detergents. Goldenseal is an herb once commonly used for infections and inflammation of the body. The herb was used for regulating healthy glands, in particular the liver, pancreas, spleen, thyroid and lymphatic system, it was also used to treat high blood pressure. Goldenseal was believed to help stimulate the body's resistance to infection. Goldenseal's strong antibiotic and antiseptic contents have been used against a wide variety of bacteria, including staph and fungi infections.

A case could be made that H. H. Holmes may have used this oil, not only to light the rooms of the "Murder Castle", but also to clean his medical instruments.

The last item from the Holmes Collection looks deceptively innocent in its current form. However, when the motives of its presence are revealed it morphs into a sinister weapon when in the hands of a murderous womanizing doctor from the south side of Chicago.

The item consists of a 5" wide by 3¼" tall piece of apothecary paper that has been hastily, yet skillfully, folded into the form of a two-sided enclosure envelope. When the envelope is unfolded an ancient dried stalk of red clover is revealed. The clover remains surprisingly intact despite that flora may have been dead for over 130 years.

So what, you say? Why is this harmless looking artifact relevant to H. H. Holmes, and more importantly, what is so sinister about it? During the Holmes era, there were as many homeopathic physicians as there were medical physicians, particularly in the rural areas of those days. While Holmes was certainly trained in all the newest, most modern medical techniques of his day, he was also well versed in homeopathic arts and herbology.

The Mystery of the H. H. Holmes Collection

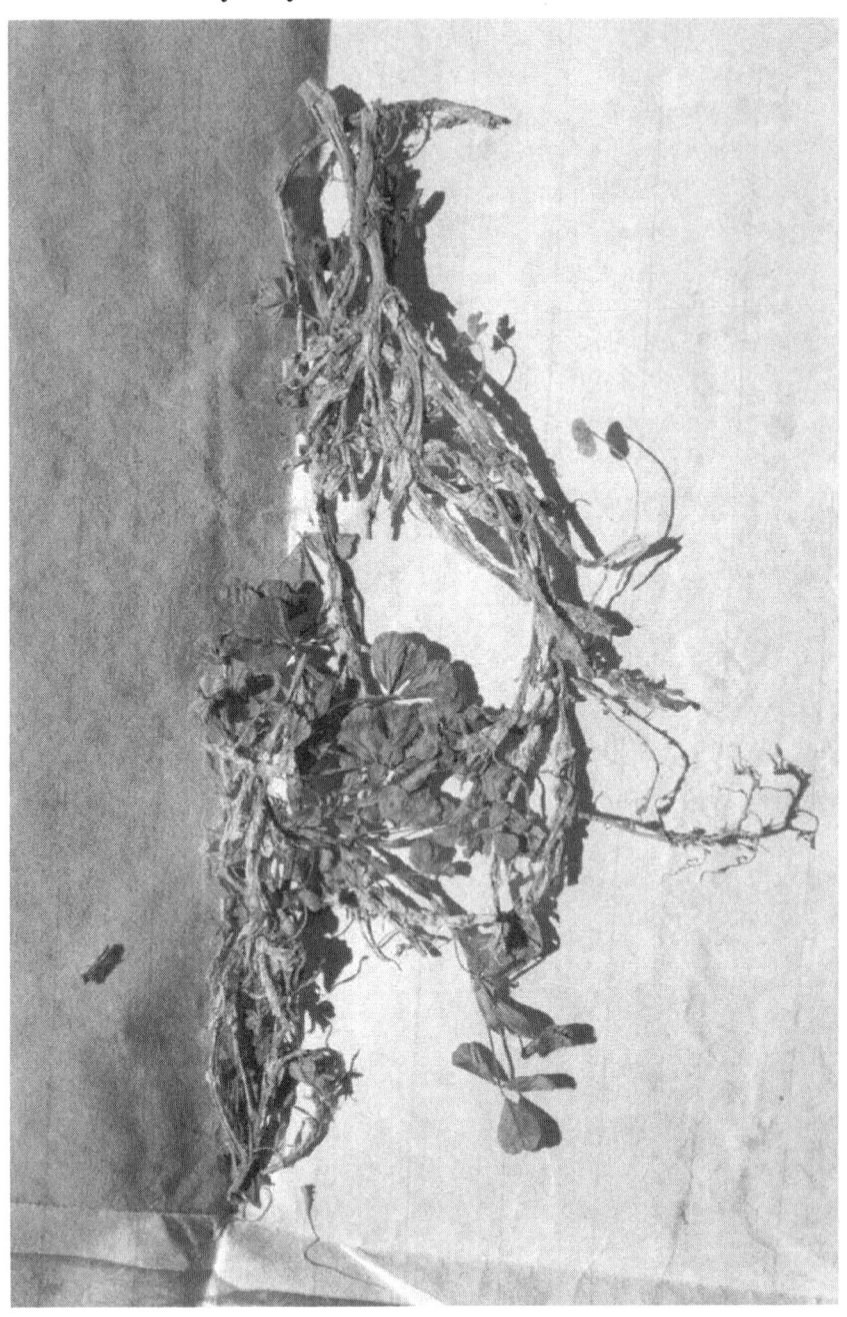

Dried red clover (Trifolium pretense), wrapped in 5" by 3¼" piece of apothecary paper.

The Mystery of the H. H. Holmes Collection

Red clover (*Trifolium pratense*) has long been promoted as a treatment for a variety of maladies, including lessening symptoms of menopause, suppressing coughs, easing disorders of the lymphatic system and treating a variety of cancers. In traditional medicine, red clover is classified as a deobstruent, antispasmodic, expectorant, sedative, anti-inflammatory, antidermatosis agent and as an abortifacient.

An abortifacient, which in Latin translates to "that which will cause a miscarriage", is a substance used to induce an abortion. Abortifacients are most often used for "mismating" animals that have mated undesirably. In humans, abortifacients were often used to terminate pregnancy up to 24 to 60 days of gestation. Their effectiveness is difficult to determine, as almost all such uses occurred before the days of clinical trials and the scientific research. Use of this type of natural abortifacient can be found in the Bible, Ancient Greek society, Aboriginal Australia, Medieval Muslim physician's records, the Catholic church and the slave colonies of pre-Civil War America.

Red clover was most often dissolved in hot tea, which masked its containment by naturally adding a slightly sweet taste to the brew. Folklore states that red clover was preferred by young women who were trying to not get pregnant, and to ease the symptoms of menstruation. Herbalists claimed that red clover was superior in getting all things "flowing" in the right direction. However, the use of red clover was ceased once the patient became pregnant.

Red clover's status as an abortifacient made it a

The Mystery of the H. H. Holmes Collection

naturally superior method of abortion for Victorian Era women. Or in this case, for men desirous of not becoming a father. Considering H. H. Holmes's unsavory reputation with the women in his life, dried red clover is exactly the sort of thing one might expect to find in his possession.

Blood Relics

Without question among the most chilling of the items found within the Holmes Collection are known amongst collectors as "blood relics". A blood relic is any item that might conceivably contain the natural DNA composition of its owner or host. There are three items contained within the Holmes Collection that could easily fit that bill.

Most prominent among them is a 5½" wide by 3" tall, Victorian era envelope that contains a lock of human

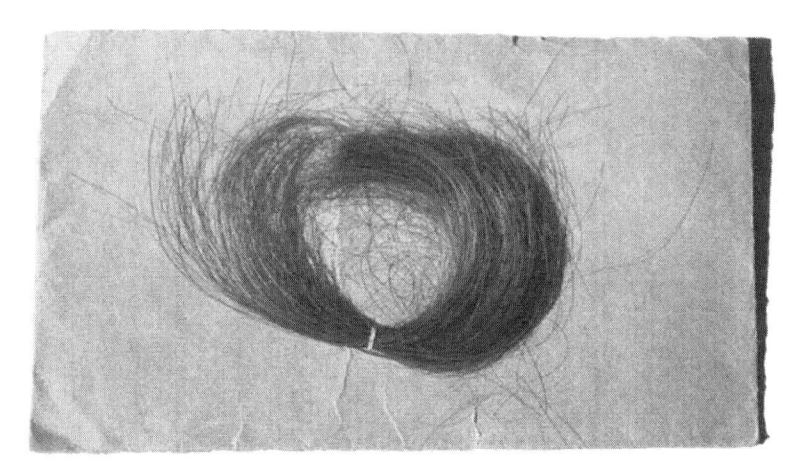

Lock of Human Hair. Approximately 3" in length, gathered in the center by a small piece of twine, wrapped in a 5½" by 3" paper.

The Mystery of the H. H. Holmes Collection

hair. The sandy brown tuft of hair is approximately 3" in length. It has been gathered in the center by a small piece of twine. At first glance it resembles a ringlet of female hair, but could just as easily be the hair from a male subject. Where did it come from? To whom did it belong? Was it a victim? A relative? The hair of a casual acquaintance or a lost love? Most likely that question will remain unanswered. Nonetheless it makes for an imaginative relic.

The next blood relic is a small (approximately ⅜" on all sides) pair of bone dice. Each individual cube has the hand-chiseled, dotted numbers on the die's six sides. Each die features the tell-tale striations that readily identify their composition as bone.

The context of their discovery within the Holmes Collection then begs the question, what type of bone is it? Although not entirely out of the question, the idea of carrying around a pair of dice made from the remains of one of his victims seems too perverse, even for Holmes. Most likely the dice are made of either ivory or whalebone, and since Holmes started life amongst the Mudgett family of

Bone Dice. Size: Approximately ⅜" on all sides.

The Mystery of the H. H. Holmes Collection

New England, he would have likely came across them as a youth. Seeing these it is easy to understand where the term "Throwing the bones" comes from in the gambling world.

Why these dice are in this collection is unknown, but it is not hard to imagine them being used to entertain the 10-year old Howard Pitezel.

Bone Awl. 4" x ½" wide x ¼" thick.

The last of the blood relics is a rather menacing looking, pointed, prehistoric looking tool also made of bone. It was hand honed by a practiced tool smith. Although Holmes was a trained medical doctor experienced in the use of all types of abject medical devices, this relic probably has a much tamer pedigree. This item is made of ivory or whalebone. It's most likely use was as an awl, used for punching holes in paper, leather, cloth and canvas, as well as for creasing paper. As unlikely as its utility may sound today, it makes perfect sense when viewed through the optics of the Victorian era. In an age well before electronic media, letter writers were the communicators of their age, often writing several letters each day.

This tool would have properly creased a letter flat in preparation for mailing, or punched a hole in several sheets so they could be strung together. For an idiosyncratic man like Holmes, it was a most functional object. Of course, when considering the source, this item could also be much more sinister in derivation and usage.

Written Artifacts

The Holmes Collection contains several miscellaneous and disjointed papers, some printed and some handwritten, that are all contemporary to the era in which the crimes occurred. Their presence makes sense in some respects, but most are destined to remain a mystery. They are frustrating to historians and researchers alike because of their random anonymity, if Holmes was a keeper of souvenirs, then these items could have meaning only to him.

One of the items is a handwritten receipt that is intriguing, when viewed in the context of H. H. Holmes's construction of his "Murder Castle" hotel in Chicago.

Building the "Castle" commenced in 1889 under the direction of Holmes himself. Holmes regularly hired and fired his construction crews, usually without payment. His frequent dismissal of architects, and construction crews, was intentionally done to protect the purpose and layout of the building. It also remains unclear whether he paid for any of the materials used to build or furnish his hotel. Given Holmes' knack for nonpayment, it is highly likely that he also neglected to pay for supplies and furnishings. Construction of the "Murder Castle" was completed in 1892, just in time for the World's Columbian

The Mystery of the H. H. Holmes Collection

Exposition of 1893 (better known as the Chicago World's Fair).

The first item is a handwritten receipt on a lined piece of paper, that looks like it may have been removed from a ledger. It reads:

Schedule A.

36 Chairs.
12 Matting and other Carpets.
5 Stoves.
1 Dining Table.
1 Hat Rack.
1 Large Mirror.
1 Sofa
3 Centre [sic] Table.
1 Fire Rug.
11 W. Stands (i.e.-wash stands).
10 Double Bed Steads and Beddings.
13 Double Bed Mattresses.
17 Pat. Springs.
2 Single Bedstead and Beddings.
2 Beauros [sic], i.e.-bureaus.
1 Small Table.
5 Bowls and Pitchers.
25 Cots Beds.

This document, appears to be designed to record the furnishings for a hotel or boardinghouse. It is easy to imagine that while these items were ordered and presumably delivered, the bill was most likely never paid for.

The next three handwritten documents in the Holmes Collection were, as was the case with the medical formulas and receipts, submitted for handwriting analysis

The Mystery of the H. H. Holmes Collection

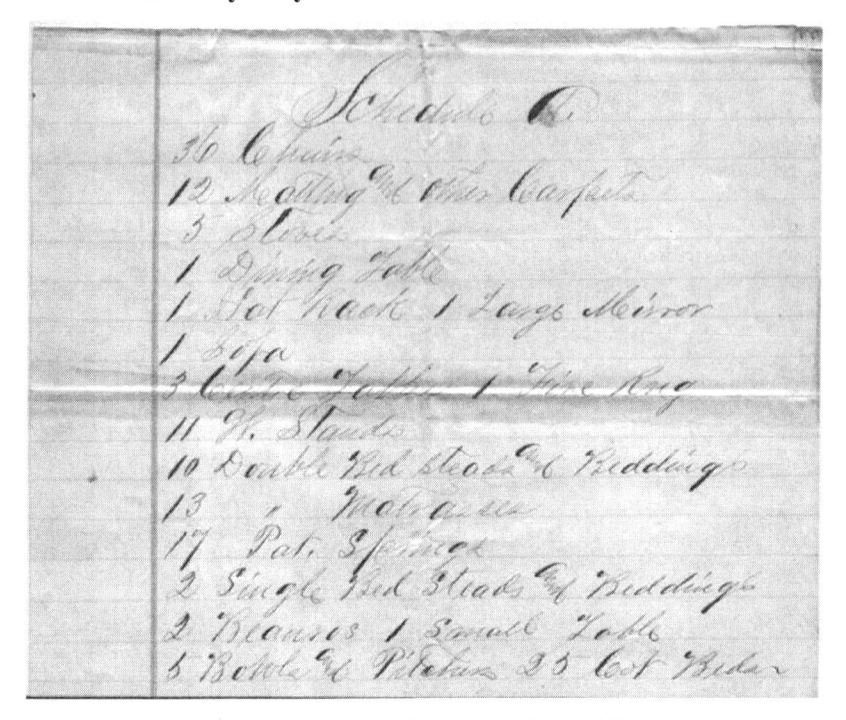

"Schedule A". 8" by 6½". Written on a piece of lined paper.

and compared to known documents written by Holmes. Once again, the results were inconclusive.

At first blush, these notes appear to be quaint little love notes written to a long-lost paramour. However, upon closer examination the first note seems quite threatening in nature.

The first one is contained on a four-inch square scrap of paper. It is handwritten but unsigned. Although there are no misspellings, the grammatical errors are accurately depicted and belong to the note's author. It reads:

Miss Margie! –

You seem to think that I am mad. When you think that you think Right, if you are with any

The Mystery of the H. H. Holmes Collection

"Miss Margie" 4" x 4". Handwritten on blank paper. Unsigned.

"No more no more" 4" x 4". Handwritten on blank paper. Unsigned.

The Mystery of the H. H. Holmes Collection

young man Friday night. Guess you had better keep it silent. You won't see me then But I may see you where you go."

The note continues on a separate, equally sized piece of paper that reads:

*"no more, no more on life's
Wide shore shall we together
Stray. Through summers
Bowers & twilight hours
when those sweet days have
past [sic] away 'twas but
a dream 'tis still a dream,
I look on heaven deep blue;
a lovely wonder far away
from heaven home & thee.
The more I love the less
it's appreciated.
You're unforgotten."*

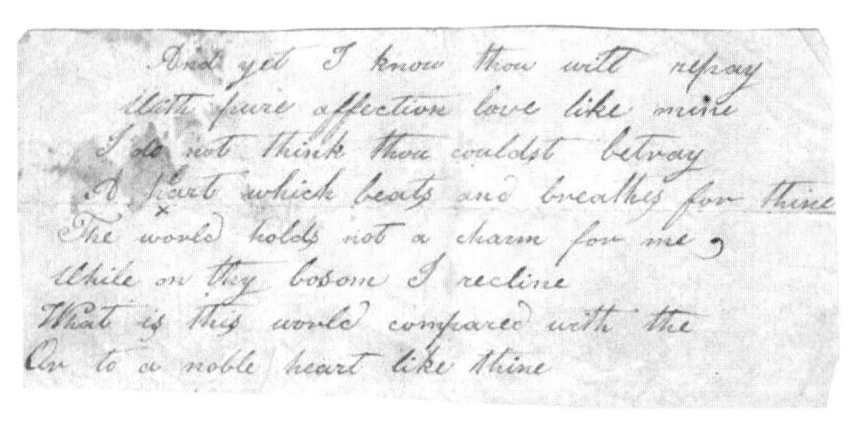

"And yet I know thou" 6½" by 3". Handwritten fragment on unlined paper. Unsigned.

The Mystery of the H. H. Holmes Collection

The third and last handwritten note is on a 6½" wide by 3" tall fragment of paper. It reads:

"And yet I know thou will repay
with pure affection love like mine.
I do not think thou couldst betray.
A heart which beats and breeze for thine.
The world holds not a charm for me,
while on the [sic](thy) bosom I recline.
What is this world compared with the [sic] (thee)
or to a noble heart like thine?

Holmes, an unrepentant and confirmed ladies' man, would most certainly have written, and received, hundreds of documents just like this throughout his adult life. While all three of these documents most certainly express affection, they all have a slightly sinister undercurrent running through them. When taken one-by-one, these notes at first convey a threat, followed by regret and close with the loss.

A psychological handwriting analysis of these three notes would key in on the descriptive words and phrases the writer uses to convey his innermost thoughts and feelings: "I am mad"… "Better keep it silent"… "You won't see me"… "No more, no more"… "Passed away"… "The less it's appreciated"… "Repay"… "Betray"… "The world holds not a charm for me". H. H. Holmes was a deviant narcissist. The tone of these notes, found as they were in a collection of his relics, reveal just what a psychopath he must have been.

An intriguing fragment of an undated note was written by J. W. Donaldson, but in 1894, Donaldson ran a drugstore in the Claypool Building in downtown Indian-

The Mystery of the H. H. Holmes Collection

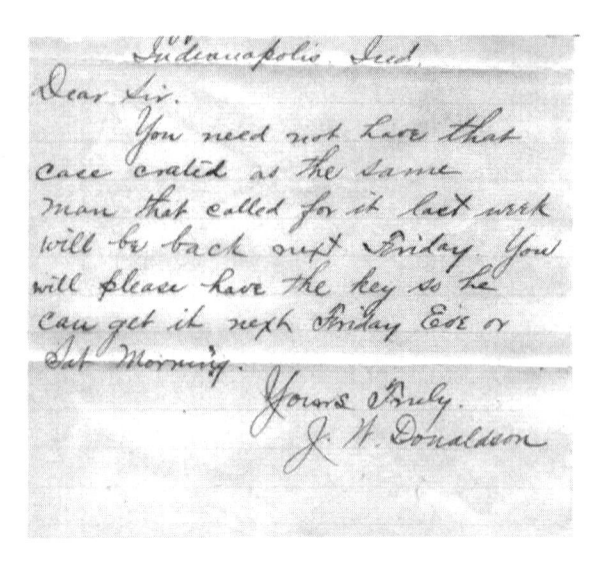

Note by J. W. Donaldson. Undated. 6" x 5.75"

apolis, just blocks from the "Circle House" Hotel where Holmes had Alice and Nellie Pitezel stashed.

The note reads:

> *"Indianapolis, Ind.*
> *Dear Sir,*
> *You need not have that case crated as the same man that called for it last week will be back next Friday. You will please have the key so he can get it next Friday Eve or Sat. Morning.*
>
> *Yours Truly,*
> *J. W. Donaldson"*

Another item found in the Holmes Collection is a 5" wide by 2¾" tall two-sided business card for The Hammond Typewriter company in Louisville Kentucky. The card features an image of the innovative looking curved front typewriter and advertises its many uses and ad- vantages for the modern business world. The Hammond

The Mystery of the H. H. Holmes Collection

Typewriter was manufactured in Chicago and first appeared on the market in 1884 while Mudgett / Holmes was graduating college.

This card is important because it fits with Holmes's reputation as a cutting-edge businessman. One of H. H. Holmes's lmost enduring schemes was promoting a copy machine to investors all over the country, and as far away as Germany. When he traveled through Irvington in October 1894, he boasted that he was on the verge of leasing several of his patent copiers to the Pennsylvania Railroad.

Holmes named his company the "A. B. C. Copier Company". It was probably the only legitimate attempt at business Holmes ever made. He described himself variously as company president, or as a "copier". Holmes was

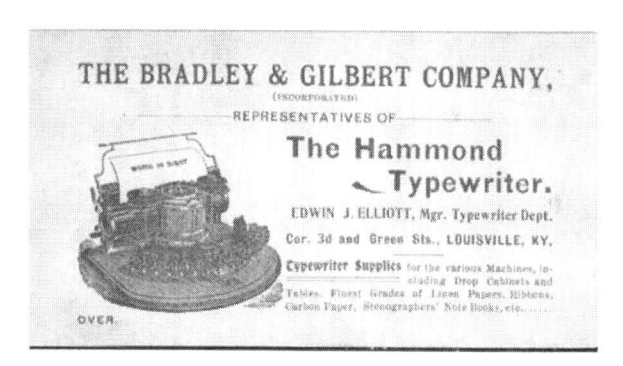

"The Bradley & Gilbert Company" Business card. 5" wide by 2¾" Front (Above), Reverse (Below)

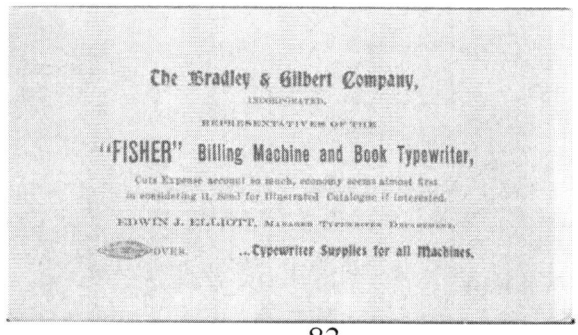

The Mystery of the H. H. Holmes Collection

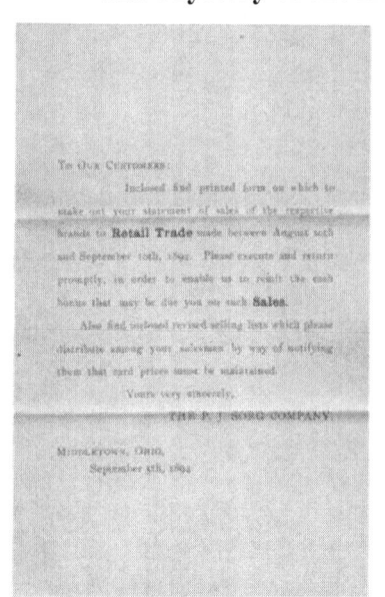

Left. "Cover letter from the P. J. Sorg Company" Dated September 5, 1894. Approximately 6" by 9".

Right. "Order form" Undated. Approximately 6" by 9".

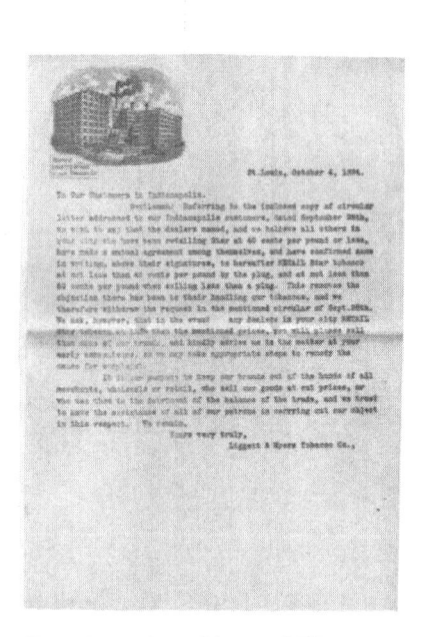

Form letter from Liggett & Myers, dated October 4, 1894.

The Mystery of the H. H. Holmes Collection

so excited about his new venture that he actually paid his very first female "typewriter" employees (as stenographers were called back then). He fell into his old habits rather quickly though by seducing and murdering all of his future "typewriters". Could this card be a memento connected to that venture?

The next item is a printed set of two forms from a Middletown Ohio cigar maker and a form letter from Liggett & Myers, all dated in the fall of 1894. This coincides with the period when H. H. Holmes was trolling around Irvington and central Indiana.

The set is approximately 6" wide by 9" tall, one is a cover letter from "The P. J. Sorg Company" of Middletown Ohio dated September 5, 1894. The cover letter refers to bulk tobacco and cigars sold to the retail trade for cash. The second page is a blank, unused order form for cigars with intriguing names like the Spear Head, Nobby Twist, Anchor, Saw Log and the Black Diamond.

Finally, the form letter from Liggett & Myers, addressed to "Our Customers in Indianapolis" also discusses the cost of tobacco products. The most intriguing aspect of this item is the date and the idea that this may have been with Holmes in Irvington. It is not hard to imagine that Holmes, ever the dapper businessman, kept his Murder Castle well stocked with cigars for his most affluent male guests and prospective victims.

There are a couple pieces of vintage ephemera both typical of the Victorian era humor and whimsy. One is a smallish cardboard trade card with a shiny metallic gold background. It features a cartoonish image of a small child carrying an American flag. There are signs that this was once pasted into a scrapbook with glue residue on the

The Mystery of the H. H. Holmes Collection

Patriotic trade card, with "Howd" written on the back in pencil.. 2" x 3".

back in all four corners. But more importantly there is a name written in pencil on the back. The name, awkwardly scrawled, spells out "Howard". Could this little trade card, typical of premiums given away by local stores before the turn of the 20th century, have belonged to 10-year-old Howard Pitezel? Could the name on the back have been written by little Howard himself?

The last item in this section is a 2½" wide by 5" tall machine printed card with a naughty little theme expressed in a ten stanza verse on front. The poem is titled "B. S." and is blank on the back. By the time you read the poem is not hard to understand what B. S. stands for.

H. H. Holmes was known to travel in a broad circle: Chicago, Indianapolis, and Cincinnati. All three cities had thriving cattle stockyards during Holmes's time and for generations after. There was a lot of money involved in the cattle trade and the slaughter houses were always located nearby. It is

The Mystery of the H. H. Holmes Collection

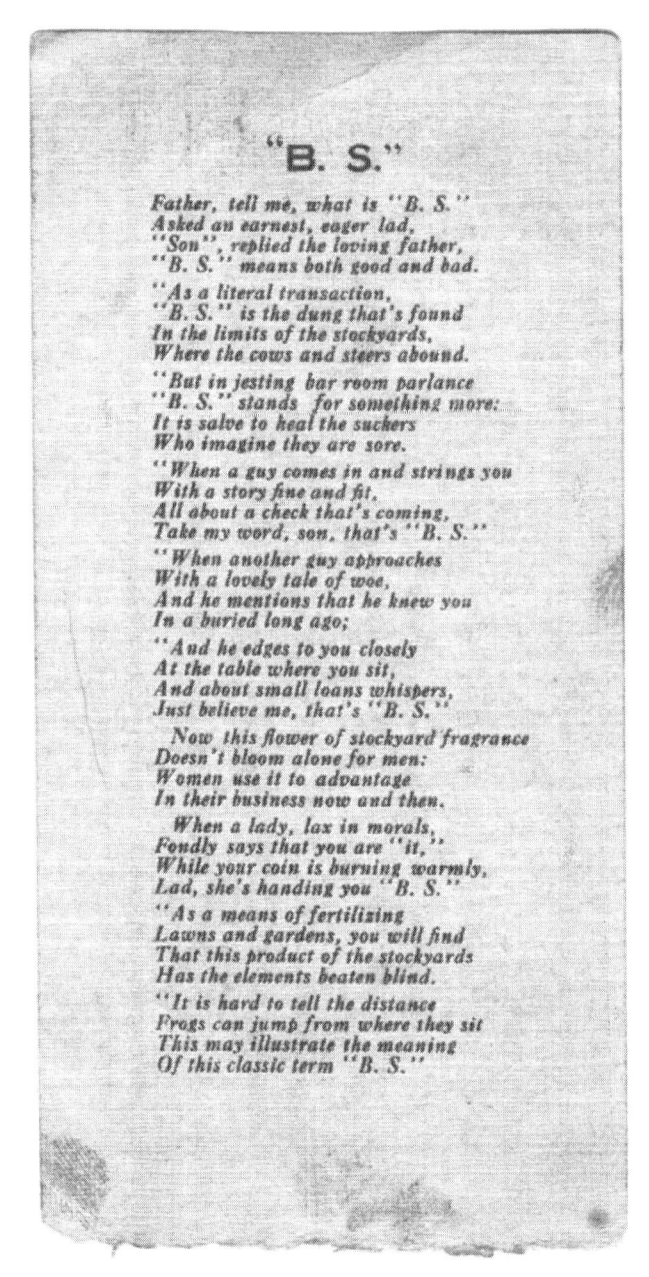

"B. S."

Father, tell me, what is "B. S."
Asked an earnest, eager lad,
"Son", replied the loving father,
"B. S." means both good and bad.

"As a literal transaction,
"B. S." is the dung that's found
In the limits of the stockyards,
Where the cows and steers abound.

"But in jesting bar room parlance
"B. S." stands for something more:
It is salve to heal the suckers
Who imagine they are sore.

"When a guy comes in and strings you
With a story fine and fit,
All about a check that's coming,
Take my word, son, that's "B. S."

"When another guy approaches
With a lovely tale of woe,
And he mentions that he knew you
In a buried long ago;

"And he edges to you closely
At the table where you sit,
And about small loans whispers,
Just believe me, that's "B. S."

Now this flower of stockyard fragrance
Doesn't bloom alone for men:
Women use it to advantage
In their business now and then.

When a lady, lax in morals,
Fondly says that you are "it,"
While your coin is burning warmly,
Lad, she's handing you "B. S."

"As a means of fertilizing
Lawns and gardens, you will find
That this product of the stockyards
Has the elements beaten blind.

"It is hard to tell the distance
Frogs can jump from where they sit
This may illustrate the meaning
Of this classic term "B. S."

"B. S." 2½" by 5". Printed on light card stock. Author unknown.

The Mystery of the H. H. Holmes Collection

not hard to imagine that Holmes would've been naturally drawn to the stockyards for both reasons.

It is equally easy to imagine that Holmes may have picked up this bawdy little card during one of those visits to entertain the precocious 10-year-old boy that was his temporary traveling companion.

The Photographs

Photography is strictly defined as the science, art, application and practice of creating durable images by capturing light and matter upon a light-sensitive material such as photographic film. Since the Holmes Collection consists of roughly 100 different of photographs, of several different types, it is important for the reader to understand the different types of photos found within. The timeline of commercial photography roughly coincides with the lifetime of H. H. Holmes, so the easiest way for us to examine their relevance is to take a look at the history of photography.

The first form of photography, available to the masses, was called a daguerreotype. This consisted of a sheet of silver-plated copper, polished to a mirror finish. The daguerreotype process debuted in Paris in 1839, and rapidly spread to America. At the height of daguerreotype's popularity in 1853, there were reportedly 86 studios in New York City alone. The daguerreotype was in use during the antebellum era, enjoying its highest popularity from 1842 to 1856. But just before the outbreak of the Civil War, daguerreotypes had fallen out of favor of a new process.

The Mystery of the H. H. Holmes Collection

In 1854, ambrotype photographs hit the market. Ambrotypes were the first real steps to introducing photography for the masses. Ambrotypes were actually negatives on glass that, when backed with a dark material, appeared as normal positive images. The drawback was, like daguerreotypes before them, ambrotypes were generally one-of-a-kind, there was no negative for making multiple copies. By the close of the Civil War ambrotypes, like some of the images they contained, faded from the scene.

By the late 1850s, the tintype and the *carte de visite* (CDV) had become the preferred method of photography for the average American family. Compared to their most important predecessor, tintypes and *carte de visite*'s were inexpensive, quick and relatively easy to make.

The tintype, also known as the ferrotype, was introduced in 1856 and used heavily until the early 1880s. Tintypes were produced on a thin metal plate, making them cheap and durable, making them easy for soldiers to carry with them on the battlefield. A photographer could prepare, expose, develop and varnish a tintype plate and have it ready for the customer in a few minutes.

A *carte de visite* was a small, credit card sized photograph pasted onto a cardboard mount. They were easier to make than a tintype and equally prized by soldiers. C*arte de visite* had a similar lifespan to tintypes (1859-1889) , but both formats were in use in rural areas well into the 1930s.

In 1866, the *carte de visite* and tintype were joined by a larger format photo known as a cabinet card, where a larger photograph was pasted onto a standard mount measuring approximately 6½" tall by 4¼" wide. The cabinet card was made using the same steps for creating *carte*

The Mystery of the H. H. Holmes Collection

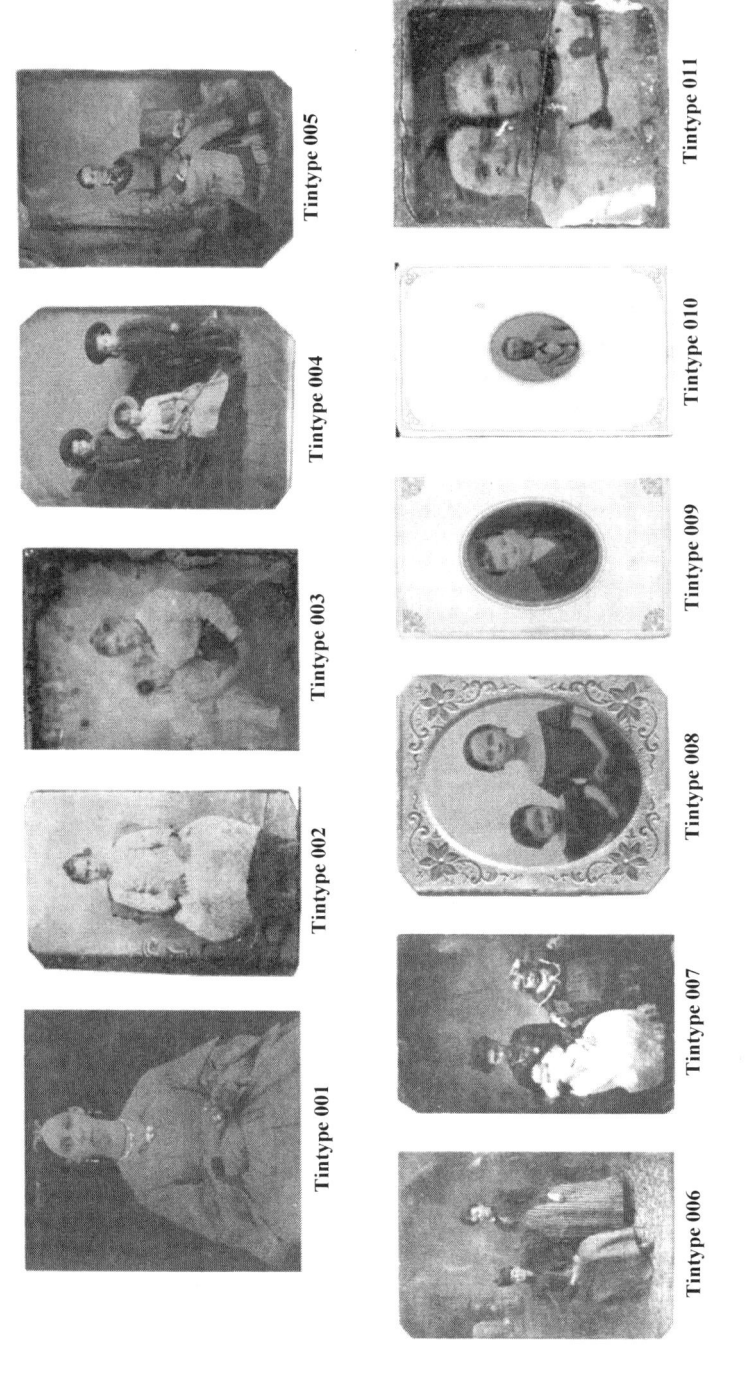

Tintype 005
Tintype 004
Tintype 003
Tintype 002
Tintype 001
Tintype 011
Tintype 010
Tintype 009
Tintype 008
Tintype 007
Tintype 006

Assorted Tintypes from the H.H. Holmes Collection
Sizes varies

91

The Mystery of the H. H. Holmes Collection

Tintype 016
Tintype 015
Tintype 014
Tintype 013
Tintype 012
Tintype 021
Tintype 020
Tintype 019
Tintype 018
Tintype 017

Assorted Tintypes from the H.H. Holmes Collection
Sizes varies

The Mystery of the H. H. Holmes Collection

Tintype 025

Tintype 024

Tintype 023

Tintype 022

Assorted Tintypes from the H.H. Holmes Collection
Sizes varies

The Mystery of the H. H. Holmes Collection

de visite and exhibited that same familiar sepia toned look. The allure of the cabinet card was that the image area was more than double the size of a *carte de visite*. By the mid-1870s, the cabinet card photograph was the preferred method of photography. Just a decade later, the advancements in photographic paper and camera equipment offered a quality level whose image clarity could rival today's digital cameras.

Many cabinet card photographs from the 1880s and 1890s are exquisite pieces of artwork, exhibiting technical excellence and wonderful composition. This new size and improved clarity provided the perfect media to showcase the grand styles of the gay nineties. The popularity of the cabinet card lasted well into the Teddy Roosevelt era.

Most of the photos found in the Holmes Collection are cabinet photos.

Sadly, the majority of the photos in the collection are not identified in any way. Some of the photographs have the names and location cities of the photography studio, where they were made, but only a few have any more information than that. Eerily the cities where the photo studios were located coincide with the travels of H. H. Holmes.

The first thing you will notice about the photos in the Holmes Collection is that smiles are grimly absent. Their somber countenance encourages assumptions of an unhappy ending. However, smiling in Victorian era photographs was considered to be low class. Humorist Mark Twain once weighed in on the subject in a letter to the **Sacramento Daily Union** on July 1, 1866, "A photograph is a most important document, and there is nothing more

The Mystery of the H. H. Holmes Collection

Assorted Card de Visite from the H.H. Holmes Collection
AApproximate size: 2.5" x 4"

The Mystery of the H. H. Holmes Collection

damning to go down to posterity than a silly, foolish smile caught and fixed forever."

People who posed for early photographs, whether earnest middle-class families recording their status for relatives and friends or celebrities captured by the lens for legions of adoring fans, understood it was a significant moment. Photography was still rare. Having your picture taken did not happen every day. For many people it was a once-in-a-lifetime experience. And in the case of these photos, the men, women and children gloomily staring back at you may well represent the only photo they ever posed for.

How beautiful and haunting these old photographs are in comparison with our modern silly selfies. Those unsmiling people probably had as much fun as we do, maybe even more. But they felt no hysterical need to prove it in their pictures. Instead, when Victorian's posed for a photograph, they thought about time, death and memory. The presence of those grave realities in old photographs makes them worthy of our interest. The possibility that they are connected to America's first serial killer demands our attention. Combined they scream, individually they cry out: find me.

The ultimate goal of displaying this collection is to attempt to start placing names to the faces, in hopes of solving the origin of the Holmes Collection. When we first acquired this group of items we had more questions than answers. The first obvious question was, why so many photographs?

One of the first steps towards answering this question came with the discovery of a copy of the *Indianapolis News* from August 28, 1895. An excerpt of that article

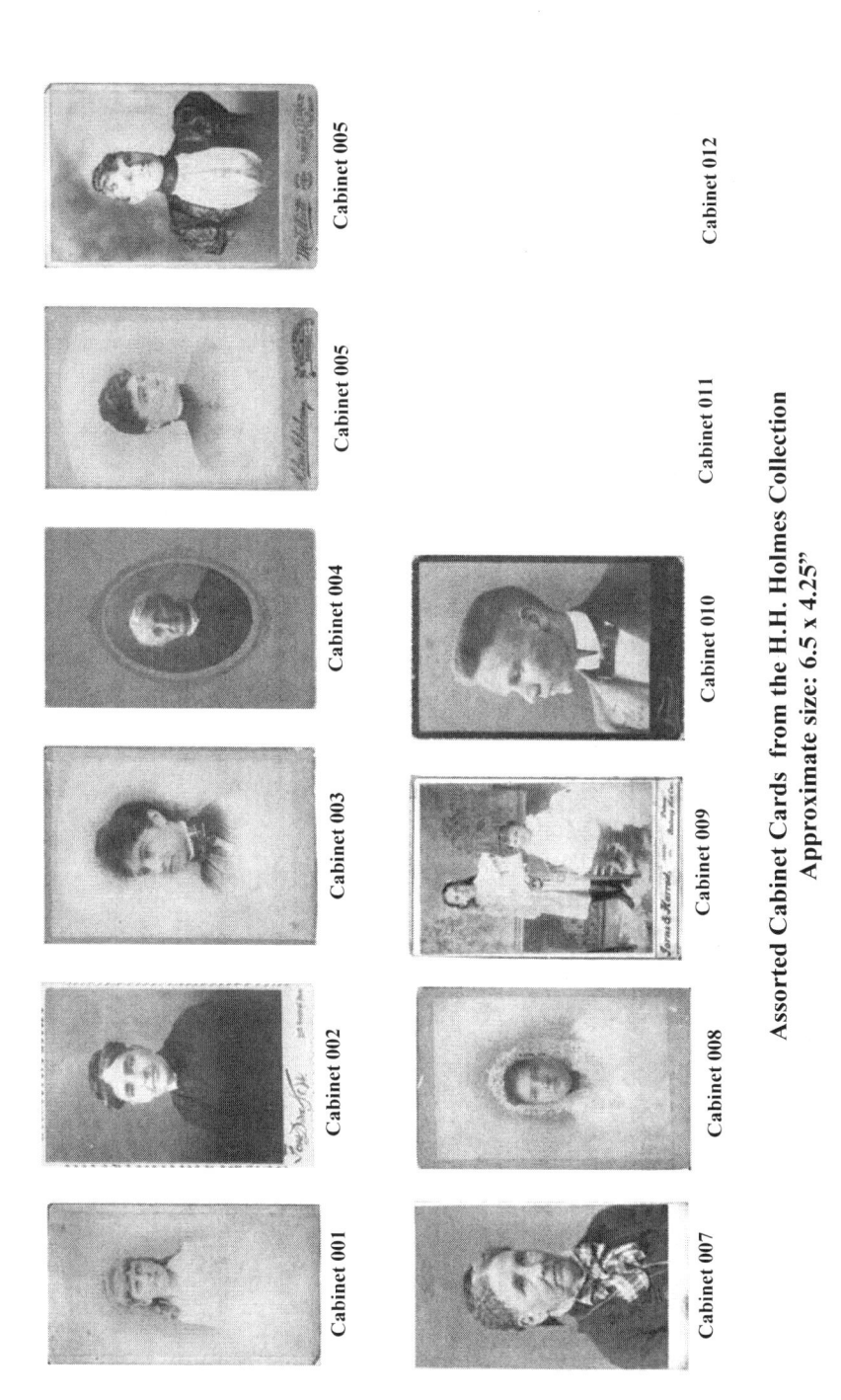

The Mystery of the H. H. Holmes Collection

Cabinet 005

Cabinet 005

Cabinet 004

Cabinet 003

Cabinet 002

Cabinet 001

Cabinet 012

Cabinet 011

Cabinet 010

Cabinet 009

Cabinet 008

Cabinet 007

Assorted Cabinet Cards from the H.H. Holmes Collection
Approximate size: 6.5 x 4.25"

The Mystery of the H. H. Holmes Collection

Cabinet 017

Cabinet 023

Cabinet 016

Cabinet 022

Cabinet 015

Cabinet 021

Cabinet 014

Cabinet 020

Cabinet 013

Cabinet 019

Cabinet 018

Assorted Cabinet Cards from the H.H. Holmes Collection
Approximate size: 6.5 x 4.25"

98

The Mystery of the H. H. Holmes Collection

Assorted Cabinet Cards from the H.H. Holmes Collection
Approximate size: 6.5 x 4.25"

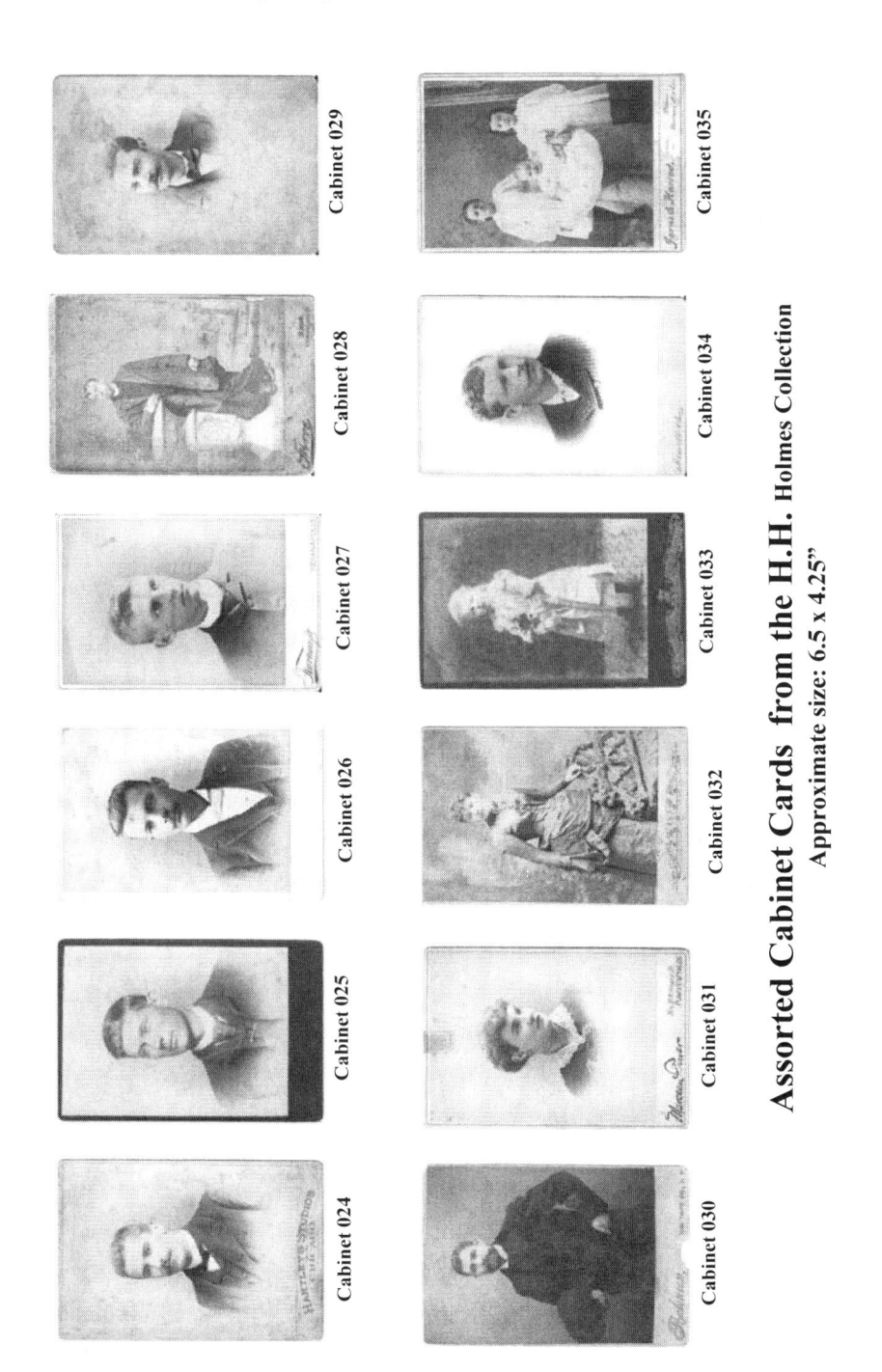

Cabinet 029
Cabinet 028
Cabinet 027
Cabinet 026
Cabinet 025
Cabinet 024
Cabinet 035
Cabinet 034
Cabinet 033
Cabinet 032
Cabinet 031
Cabinet 030

The Mystery of the H. H. Holmes Collection

Cabinet 041
Cabinet 040
Cabinet 039
Cabinet 038
Cabinet 037
Cabinet 036
Cabinet 047
Cabinet 046
Cabinet 045
Cabinet 044
Cabinet 043
Cabinet 042

Assorted Cabinet Cards from the H.H. Holmes Collection
Approximate size: 6.5 x 4.25"

100

The Mystery of the H. H. Holmes Collection

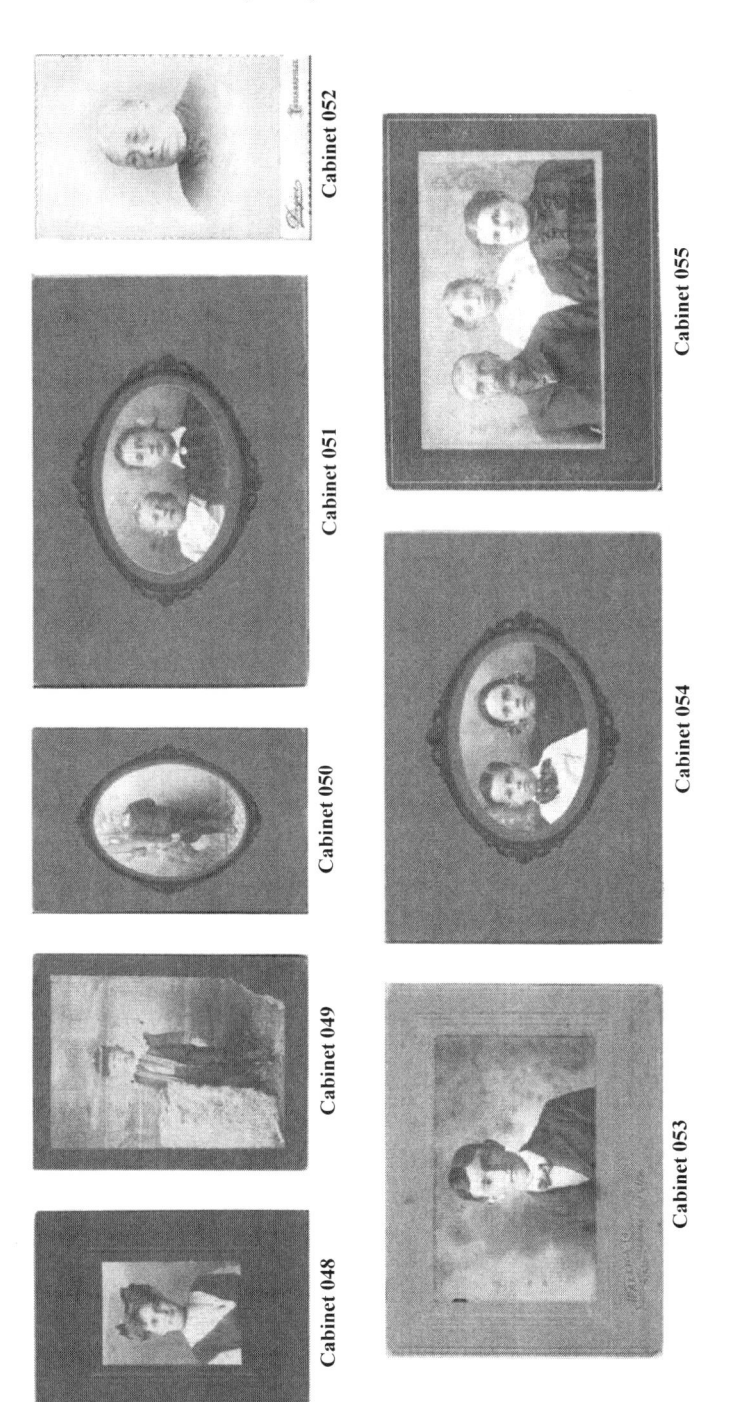

Cabinet 052
Cabinet 051
Cabinet 050
Cabinet 049
Cabinet 048
Cabinet 055
Cabinet 054
Cabinet 053

Assorted Cabinet Cards from the H.H. Holmes Collection
Approximate size: 6.5 x 4.25"

The Mystery of the H. H. Holmes Collection

Cabinet 058

Cabinet 057

Cabinet 056

Assorted Cabinet Cards from the H.H. Holmes Collection
Approximate size: 6.5" x 4.25"

The Mystery of the H. H. Holmes Collection

about Holmes's time in Irvington reads:

When Doctor Thompson moved out he left some furniture in the house, including a stove and carpet. The man, giving his name as Laws, said that he wanted the house for his sister, Mrs. Cook, who would live there with her three children, and would conduct a boarding house...The man also rented a lockbox at the post office for two weeks, and received a great amount of mail, the greater portion of it being photographs and tintype pictures. He received this mail for several days. Then it suddenly stopped coming, and none has come for him since."

Another reference to photographs in the H. H. Holmes saga can be found in the 1896 book, **The Holmes – Pitezel Case. A History of the Greatest Crime of the Century And of the Search for the Missing Pitezel Children** by Detective Frank Geyer. In Chapter 17, titled "When He Came", Geyer wrote:

"...in the barn I found a large coal stove, called the 'Peninsular Oak,' and some other articles of furniture. The stove was three and a half feet high, and twenty-two inches in diameter, – the entire top working upon a pivot. On the top I found what appeared to be blood stains... In the chimney we also found some of the iron fastenings which belong to the (boy's) trunk, some buttons, a small scarf pen, and a crochet needle."

The next day the local newspapers also reported that the remains of several charred photographs and tintypes were found among the ashes.

Further evidence exists that H. H. Holmes had a

The Mystery of the H. H. Holmes Collection

Photos from the photo album containing the autopsy class photo.

104

The Mystery of the H. H. Holmes Collection

Photos from the photo album containing the autopsy class photo.

105

The Mystery of the H. H. Holmes Collection

Photos from the photo album containing the autopsy class photo.

The Mystery of the H. H. Holmes Collection

thing for photos. When the police discovered the trunk in which he killed Anna Williams, which Holmes had thrown into Lake Michigan, all that was left inside was a tintype photo and a "bangle" made of 3-cent pieces, The photo was reported to be of the victim, and the bracelet was said to have belonged to her as well.

During the making of the *American Ripper* TV program a facial recognition expert identified the small framed tintype contained in the Holmes Collection as being an image of Jack the Ripper's third victim Elizabeth "Long Liz" Stride (November 27, 1843 – September 30, 1888).

On the night before her murder, September 29, Stride was seen wearing a black jacket and skirt com-

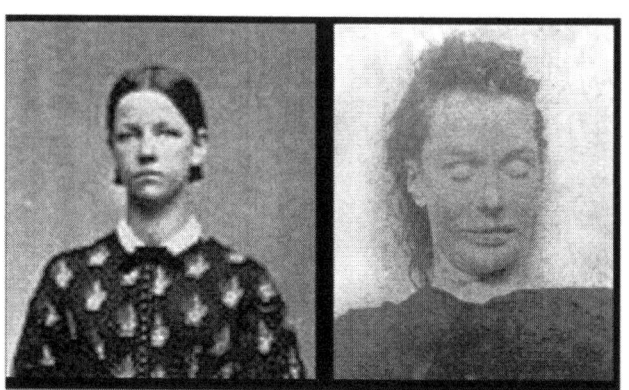

A confirmed photograph of a young Ripper victim, Elizabeth Stride (left) and her autopsy photo (right)

The Mystery of the H. H. Holmes Collection

plemented by a black crêpe bonnet. She was also seen with a client, a man with a dark moustache wearing a bowler hat, at around 11:00 p.m. Stride's body was discovered close to 1 a.m. on Sunday September 30. 1888. With blood still flowing from a wound in her neck, it appeared that she was killed just moments before her body was discovered. It is possible that the killer was interrupted before he had the opportunity to mutilate the body.

No purse or handbag was found on Stride's body, so it is likely that her night's "earnings", along with any personal effects, were removed from her body by her murderer. It is plausible that this photo may have been contained in that purse or handbag. If Jeff Mudgett's theory that his Great-great-grandfather H.H. Holmes was also Jack the Ripper is correct, the presence of this photo among the artifacts strengthens his case.

The inquest into the murder of Long Liz Stride was opened on October 1, 1888 by coroner, Wynne Edwin Baxter. Coroner Baxter believed that Stride had been attacked with "a swift, sudden action... the murderer could have taken advantage of a checked scarf she was wearing to grab her from behind before slitting her throat." The coroner further stated that, unlike the previous Ripper murders, the blade used to kill Liz Stride might have been shorter and of a different design. The two scalpels that were made in England and found within the Holmes Archive Collection would fit the coroner's description.

The true mystery of the Holmes Collection may well rest somewhere in these photos. While the possibility of including a photo of a Ripper victim is intriguing, the most enigmatic may be the photos found in the same period photo album as the autopsy photo shown on page 45. Like the other pictures in this mix, they are as interesting as they are beautiful, and raise more questions than they answer. Who are these people? What is their connection to H. H. Holmes? Are they victims, family, acquaintances, accomplices or friends? Were they given to Holmes as keepsakes, or were they taken by Holmes as souvenirs?

The Mystery of the H. H. Holmes Collection

In the context of the rest of the Holmes Collection, it seems obvious that this group of items once belonged to America's first serial killer, H. H. Holmes. The possibility that they are connected to America's first serial killer demands our attention. Combined they scream, individually they cry out: find me! To do that, we need your help.

The Mystery of the H. H. Holmes Collection

Part Three

Suspects and The Holmes Curse

The Mystery of the H. H. Holmes Collection

The Curse of H. H. Holmes

Understanding Holmes, what he did and why he did it, is hard enough but understanding the aftermath is even harder. While the origin of the Holmes Collection is unknown, there can be no doubt that it is now part of the aftermath. The most well-known aspect of the H. H. Holmes aftermath is known as "The Holmes Curse" and may be the reason why this collection of artifacts remained underground for a century or more. So it may be best if we start our investigation by learning the details of "The Holmes Curse".

The Holmes's curse began well before his execution. Holmes himself was the first to identify the curse while stewing behind bars in Philadelphia's Moyamensing prison. In what must surely be one of the earliest examples of tabloid "pay-for-play" journalism, H. H. Holmes was paid $7,500 (over $213,000 in today's money) by the Hearst newspapers his written confession.

He wrote:

"I am convinced that since my imprisonment I have changed woefully and gruesomely from what I was formerly in feature and figure. My features are as-

The Mystery of the H. H. Holmes Collection

suming a pronounced satanical cast... My head and face are gradually assuming an elongated shape. I was born with the evil one standing as my sponsor beside the bed where I was ushered into the world, and he has been with me since....I believe fully that I am growing to resemble the devil – that the similitude is almost completed."

In October 1895, one year after his murderous walk through Irvington, Holmes was tried for the murder of Benjamin Pitezel, the father of Irvington victim, Howard Pitezel. Holmes was subsequently found guilty and sentenced to death on November 30th and hanged on May 7, 1896, at Moyamensing County Prison. Until the moment of his death, Holmes showed few signs of fear, anxiety or depression.

Holmes last evil act came as he stood before the trap door of the gallows, denying everything.

"Gentlemen," he said, ".... I only want to say that the extent of my wrong doings in the taking of human life consisted in the death of two women, ...that I am not guilty of taking the lives of any of the Pietzel [sic] family, the three children or the father, Benjamin F Pietzel [sic], of whose death I am now convicted, and for which I am today to be hanged. That is all."

Holmes then stepped forward and stood upon the trap door and remarked, "Take your time; don't bungle it." As the cap was adjusted, the hangman asked, "Are you ready?" Holmes replied quietly, "Yes, good-bye," and the trap was sprung. Although the trap was sprung precisely at 10:12:30, Holmes' neck was not broken, and the next 15 minutes were filled with "convulsive twitches of the

The Mystery of the H. H. Holmes Collection

limbs and painful gasps for breath" before Holmes was pronounced dead. This gruesome detail leads conspiratorialists to believe that H. H. Holmes swore a cursed for the devil to punish any and all those who brought him to this end.

    The body was not cut down until 10:45. When it was laid out on the stretcher, it was discovered that the knot was badly jammed. The doctors failed to loosen it as they attempted to remove the noose from his neck. Finally it was decided to cut the rope, but Superintendent Perkins objected and the knot was finally undone after several minutes of trying work.

    The body was immediately placed in a plain pine coffin, wide enough and deep enough to have held two men of Holmes' size. An undertaker's wagon conveyed it to the receiving vault. The only persons at the cemetery were the undertaker and his assistant, two grave-diggers, two watchmen and a couple of newspaper men. This small

The unmarked grave of Herman Mudgett in Holy Cross Cemetery, Yeadon, Pennsylvania, Photo by Karen Valentine, https://www.findagrave.com

The Mystery of the H. H. Holmes Collection

group was pressed into service as pallbearers and witnessed H. H. Holmes' last macabre request. Once in the temporary vault, the lid of the coffin was taken off, the body lifted out and laid on the ground. The bottom of the coffin was filled with cement, the body was replaced inside and then covered by a second layer of cement. Holmes' intended that this cement would harden around his body and prevent any attempt at grave robbery. The coffin was left in the receiving vault all night under the guard of two watchmen, while the mixture hardened.

The following events have been attributed to the Holmes Curse:

- The day after young Howard Pitezel was killed, on October 11, 1894, George W. Powell, the Superintendent of the Indianapolis police force, and the man in charge of the Circle City chase for H. H. Holmes was participating in a parade to dedicate the Knights of Pythias Hall in Lebanon, Indiana. He was thrown from his horse, hitting his head against a curb. For a time, it was thought he would not survive, but he eventually recovered. He dealt with the after effects of the injury for the rest of his life.

- Dr. William K. Martin, a coroner's physician who had been a major witness against Holmes at the trial was the first person to die. He dropped dead at his post in in the coroner's office from blood poisoning on April 17, 1896, shortly before Holmes was hung on May 7, 1896.

- Michael Arnold, the trial judge, and Dr. Ashbridge, the lead coroner, were both stricken with a previously undiagnosed, deadly illnesses.

The Mystery of the H. H. Holmes Collection

- Howard Perkins, the prison superintendent at Moyamensing, where Holmes spent his final days and who presided over Holmes's execution, committed suicide by shooting himself in the head.

- The father of one of Holmes' victims was horribly burned in a gas explosion.

- The remarkably healthy Pinkerton agent, Frank Geyer, suddenly became seriously ill after Holmes' execution. Thankfully though, the diligent detective pulled through.

- The office of the claims manager for one of the insurance companies that Holmes had cheated, caught fire and burned. Everything in the office was destroyed except for a framed copy of Holmes' arrest warrant and two portraits of the killer.

- Mrs. Anna Harvey of Chicago, who lived in the "Murder Castle", committed suicide.

- Holmes's lawyer, Samuel P. Rotan's fiancé of died suddenly.

- The priest who had prayed with Holmes before his execution was found dead in the church courtyard. The coroner ruled the death as uremic poisoning but according to reports, his body was found badly beaten and robbed.

- Linford L. Biles, the jury foreman, was electrocuted in a strange accident involving power lines above his house.

- On New Year's Eve 1909, the "Handsome Bandit" Marion Hedgepeth, who had been pardoned for informing on cellmate H. H. Holmes, was shot and killed by police officer Edward Jaburek during a holdup at a Chicago

The Mystery of the H. H. Holmes Collection

saloon at 18th and Avers Avenue.

- The residents of the "Holmes' House" in Irvington also suffered from more than their share of troubles.
    - Early in 1895, R. R. Miles bought the Julian Avenue house for $3,000 and it continued to be rented after Holmes left.
    - In the fall of 1900, Rev. Charles Fisk Beach bought this Irvington house and lot for $3,500 and resided there for about a year before selling the property at a 20% loss. No reason was ever given for taking the loss.
    - John Monroe Connell acquired the "Holmes House" and the large lot in the summer of 1903. In July 1904, tragedy befell Connell when his son, Jack, drowned while canoeing with friends at Broad Ripple. Three years later, Connell's marriage failed. He gave up his business and became a road superintendent for Barber Asphalt Paving Co.
    - Edward Branham and his family lived in the house for a short time, but complained of foul odors emanating from the cellar. Lime was spread around the foundation, but the odor persisted. Edward Branham died on October 15, 1906 from injuries he received when struck by an automobile while attempting to cross Illinois and Michigan Streets.
    - Folie G. Hamilton, who lived briefly in the "Holmes House," died of lobar pneumonia in 1907 at age 35.

The Mystery of the H. H. Holmes Collection

Then there is the mysterious fate of the house itself. For generations, local lore claimed that over the course of a few years in the early 20th century, the original house was torn apart by Butler College students forced to spend the night in the infamous house as part of a hazing ritual.

Don Flick, President of the Irvington Historic Society, explains that the original house, known after 1894 as the "Holmes Cottage", was moved to a new location around the turn of the century. "The house in which H.H. Holmes killed Howard Pitezel in October 1894 - was originally the only house on the half-block bounded by Julian Avenue on the north, Good Avenue on the east, the Pennsy Trail on the south, and the north-south alley to the west. The house sat in the center of the lot, and the front of the house faced Julian, which is substantiated by maps from that time."

Don continues, "Several years after the events surrounding the Howard Pitezel murder, the property was purchased by a developer named Brydon who subdivided the large single lot into eight smaller lots - three facing Julian and five facing Good. Because the existing house was located in the center of the subdivision, Brydon had the house lifted from its foundation, rotated so that the front of the house faced east, set on a new foundation on Lot 4 of the subdivision (the closest lot to the original location of the house), and given the address 114 S. Good Avenue."

"When Brydon obtained permits for the subdivision, he obtained seven new construction building permits for seven new houses, as well as one remodeling permit for an existing house, thus substantiating that one of the eight houses that make up the subdivision was existing at

The Mystery of the H. H. Holmes Collection

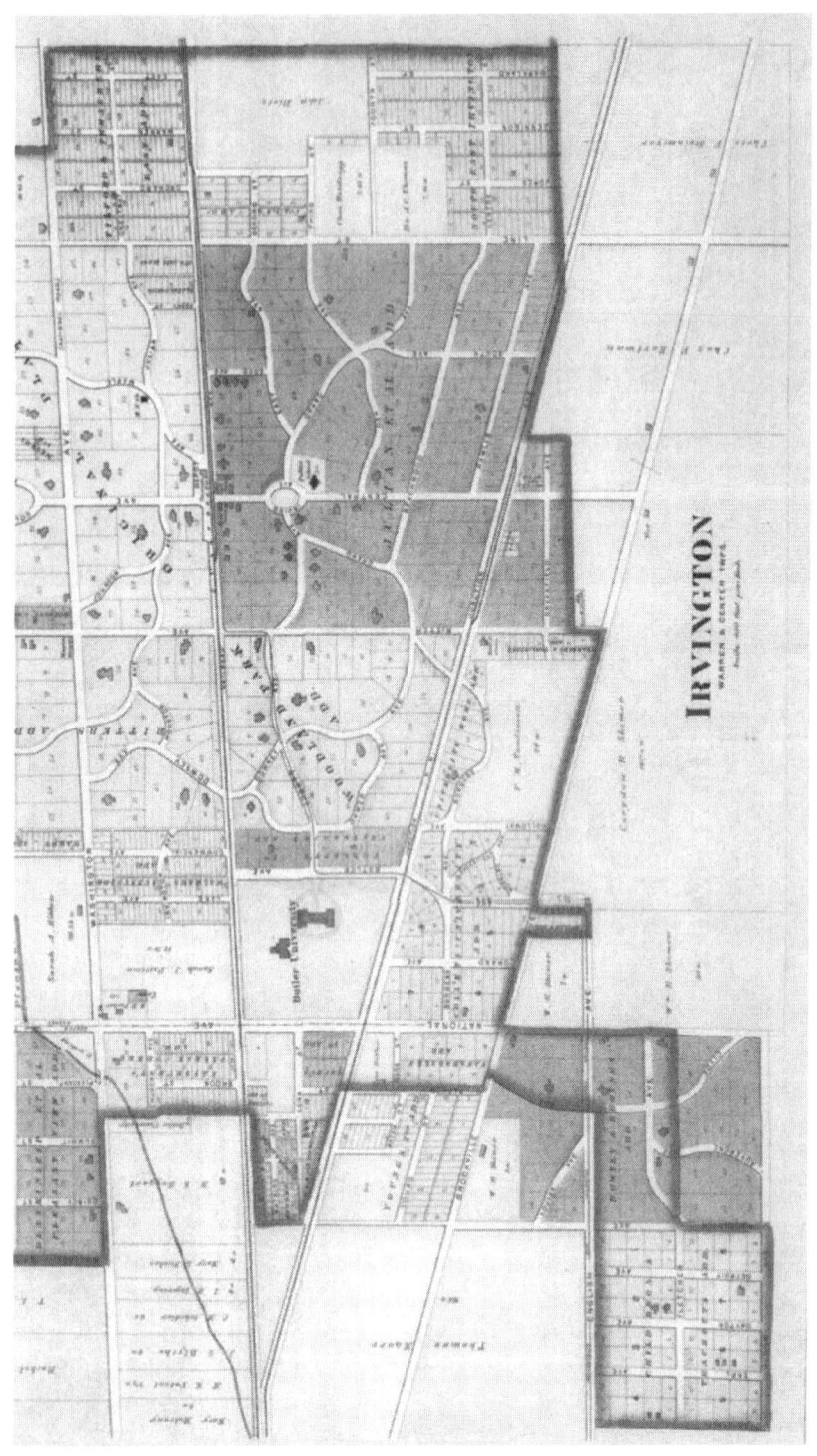

The Mystery of the H. H. Holmes Collection

the time of Brydon's purchase, and which could only have been the Holmes house This relocation of the house is further substantiated by photographic verification of similarities between the Holmes house in 1895 and the current house at 114 S. Good. " says Don Flick.

When asked how, physically, the house was moved back then, Don explains, "Holes were cut into the original foundation walls just under the floor joists, beams were installed across the house, the beams were raised by jacks, the foundation walls were removed, some type of wheeled rig/trailer/truck bed was slid under the house, it was pulled, rotated, and moved above a new foundation at the new location, and the house lowered onto the new foundation. Despite all the work involved, this was not an uncommon thing to do at the time."

Holmes's Chicago "Murder Castle" also seemed to be cursed. It was mysteriously gutted by fire in August 1895. According to a newspaper clipping from the New York Times, two men were seen entering the back of the Castle around 8 to 9 p.m. About a half an hour later, witnesses saw them run from the building in a dead sprint. Their hasty retreat was quickly followed by several explosions and within moments, the building was in flames. Afterwards, investigators found a half-empty gas can underneath the back steps of the building.

Some believed that the Castle fire was started to destroy any remaining evidence that the police hadn't discovered yet. Others speculated that outraged neighbors set fire to it to prevent the "Castle" from becoming a future tourist attraction. There is evidence for the latter, on August 5, 1895, a carnival sideshow exhibition known as "Kohl & Middleton's Clark Street Dime Museum" opened

The Mystery of the H. H. Holmes Collection

featuring an exhibition centered around Holmes. The brochure advertised:

> "H. H. Holmes! Come and see a lifelike representation in wax of this most noted criminal. Suspect of modern times. This figure is the work of the most skilled artists in America, who have been engaged for weeks in modeling a perfect counterfeit presentment of this alleged Wholesale Murderer of Men, Women and Innocent Children! Many interesting relics of Holmes and his supposedly victims."

Despite the attempted arson, the building at 63rd & Wallace on Chicago's rough Southside survived the fire and remained in use until it was demolished in 1938.

The site is currently occupied by the Englewood branch of the United States Postal Service. The Holmes curse lingered in Englewood long after the 1893 Chicago World's Fair and Holmes' death. Today, the three-square mile neighborhood is one of the most dangerous neighborhoods in Chicago. Plagued by crime, drugs, gang activity, and violence, it suffers from a number of serious problems afflicting poor inner-city communities across the United States.

The idea that the Holmes Collection might somehow be connected to the Holmes Curse may be found in the possible ownership suspects we will consider on the pages that follow. While there can be no doubt that his victims were cursed by their untimely demise, the curse of H.H. Holmes continued to claim victims long after he was gone.

The Mystery of the H. H. Holmes Collection

Tracking down the Collection's Creator

As detailed earlier in this volume, the origin of this collection is a total mystery. We received it in 2004 from an unnamed, elderly couple who had attended one of our Greenfield, IN tours. According to my brief conversation with them, the collection belonged to "a relative" and that they "just wanted it gone." After I expressed an interest in the collection, they disappeared, only to drop a box off anonymously a week later. In the decade and a half since that time, it is likely that one or both of these mysterious benefactors has passed away, so the collections true provenance may never be determined.

It seems obvious from examining the collection, that this group of items belonged to America's first serial killer, H. H. Holmes, or someone with a close interest or relationship to him. In this part of this volume, I will review my short list of suspects who may have owned it. There are several possibilities, some obvious, and some obscure. I have attempted to identify the possible owners through biographies, personal connections or susceptibility. I invite you to form your own theory of ownership.

Charles W. Miller

I believe that the Holmes Collection belonged to a Greenfield lawyer and Indianapolis judge named Charles W. Miller. I base my conclusion on few things.

One of the photographs in the Holmes Collection is a cabinet photo of a well-dressed young man taken at the Lewis & Gibson studio in Ann Arbor, Michigan.

Lewis & Gibson was the official photography studio for the University of Michigan during the 1880s. The Mudgett family retains a well published photo of young Herman Webster Mudgett taken during his senior year, which is identical in style to the photo of Miller. There are also two other cabinet photos of pretty, young women on the same style of backer board identical to the Miller and Mudgett photos.

Miller graduated from Michigan Law School the same year that Mudgett graduated from Medical School (1884). The photo is autographed on the reverse side, a

The Mystery of the H. H. Holmes Collection

1884 University of Michigan Graduation Cabinet Cards. Center: Charles W. Miller. Left and Right: Unknown.

The Mystery of the H. H. Holmes Collection

common Victorian era custom between classmates that exists to the present day. The photo is signed "Very Truly Yours, Chas. W. Miller K.K.K. Law of '84 U. of M.".

[Editors Note: The ominous sounding, the K.K.K. added to Miller's signature refers to the Kappa Kappa Kappa Fraternity, known colloquially as "Tri-Kap," or K.K.K. The fraternity was founded in 1842, 24 years before the Ku Klux Klan first started.]

Although Charles W. Miller's name does not appear alongside his classmate in the 1884 University of Michigan graduation program found elsewhere in the collection, the pair most likely knew each other. Given Holmes's penchant for committing crimes as a matter of routine, it seems likely that the budding young conman would cozy up to the budding young lawyer. A friend like Miller could come in handy someday. I believe another explanation for ownership of the Holmes Collection can be found in the personal biography of Charles W. Miller himself.

The Goshen, Indiana born Miller graduated with a L.L.D. law degree in 1884. The L.L.D. is awarded to esablished scholars who have given "proof of distinction by some original contribution to the advancement of the

The Mystery of the H. H. Holmes Collection

science or study of law". Miller opened a law practice in Greenfield, Indiana, the same year he graduated. From 1888 to 1890, he took a break from his law practice to serve as Mayor of his hometown of Goshen.

For the next decade, Miller practiced law in central Indiana. Not much is known about counselor Miller during the time his classmate was committing murders. He was elected Attorney General of Indiana from 1903 to 1907 and served as U.S. Attorney for the State of Indiana from 1909 to 1914. As U.S. Attorney, Miller presided over the famed dynamite trials in Indianapolis. These trials involved the early labor union movement in America and quickly gained countrywide attention, and eventually involved national names like Samuel Gompers, Eugene V. Debs and lawyer Clarence Darrow. It seemed that Charles W. Miller had the world by the tail. Then, like the collection itself, things got strange.

On Friday, February 16, 1923, sometime before 5:00 pm, Miller checked into Room 117 of the English Hotel on Monument Circle in Indianapolis. He had just returned from an early afternoon trip to the Hook's Drug Store at Market and Pennsylvania Streets. The store clerk recalled that Miller had purchased a straight razor, and a bottle of carbolic acid, a poison also known as Phenol. Carbolic acid was a disinfectant most often found in soap. After entering the hotel, Miller greeted the doorman and retired to his room, bolting the door behind him.

Once alone, Miller removed his hat and overcoat, taking care to arrange them neatly atop a nearby chair. He carefully removed his stiff starched collar and necktie, and meticulously placed them atop a nearby writing table. Miller removed the lid from the bottle of carbolic acid and

The Mystery of the H. H. Holmes Collection

drank the contents. He then picked up the straight razor, gazed at his own im- age staring back from the mirror atop the dresser, and slit his own throat.

The next morning, Miller failed to show up for a meeting with businessman Ira T. Swartz of the Swartz-Gasser Company. The hotel was alerted and asked to check on the judge's welfare. The clerks got no response from repeated knocks on the door, so the police were called. When Indianapolis police detectives Stewart and Gauglin arrived at the Hotel English, they found in the register a badly scrawled name which was deciphered as that of Mr. Miller. They found the hotel room door bolted from the inside and got no response from the resident within.

The detectives finally gained entrance to Miller's room via an exterior window. Inside they found Miller's body lying on the floor near the foot of the bed. A razor covered with blood lay on the dresser nearby. In front of the dresser was a small rug saturated with blood. A half pint bottle containing traces of carbolic acid was found in the cuspidor (spittoon).

Marion County coroner, Dr. Paul F. Robinson, who examined the body on Saturday evening, said either the poison or the wound would have produced death. Friends attributed Mr. Miller's act to a nervous breakdown result- ing from overwork. Lucius O. Hamilton, of North Ala- bama Street, and a friend of the family, said that Mr. Mil- ler had been extremely nervous in the days before his passing. Mr. Miller had been working night and day for some time, and his breakdown was without doubt the re- sult of overwork.

"Mr. Miller was sixty years old," Mr. Dowling,

The Mystery of the H. H. Holmes Collection

another family friend said, "at a time in his life when he should have been slowing down instead of speeding up. He couldn't stand the strain of additional work which he took on himself, in the acquisition of some important legal cases by the firm." Mr. Dowling said that Mr. Miller had not acted differently on the day of his disappearance than he had on any other day for the last few weeks, but had busied himself with work at the office until his usual time for leaving, and had talked with a client from Terre Haute a few minutes before leaving the office that last day.

Three days later, funeral services for Charles W. Miller, were held in St. James Episcopal church at Goshen, his former hometown. He was buried in Oakridge cemetery at Goshen.

Here was a man who had reached the pinnacle of the legal profession. Respected, revered and financially well-off, his record was clean. But something was bothering him. If the supposition that Miller and Mudgett were friends is true, then a strong case can be made that the Holmes Collection belonged to Judge Miller.

During Holmes's decade of debauchery, Miller was building a career as a lawyer in Greenfield, twenty miles east of Indianapolis. The only break in the timeline were the two years when Miller served as Mayor of Goshen, a northern Indiana town resting on an almost parallel line with Chicago. As we will see later in this volume,

H. H. Holmes had many ties to Indiana. Perhaps Charles W. Miller was one of those ties.

Culturally, there may be a deeper reason that the Holmes Collection assemblage may rest with Miller. Suicide in Victorian America was extremely taboo. As late as

The Mystery of the H. H. Holmes Collection

World War II, suicide was viewed as unchristian; It was the ultimate sin. In those days, when a relative died by his or her own hand, their name was inked out of the familial conscience. In the family home, pictures were removed, possessions were boxed up to be stored away forever and sometimes, the bedrooms of the departed were sealed, never to be occupied again. Although Miller died during the Roaring Twenties, he was born and raised a Victorian when suicide demanded suppression and quick entombment. Miller was found dead on Saturday afternoon, his body shipped up to Goshen and he was in the ground less than 72 hours later.

Without question, the Miller family name appears repeatedly in this collection. The Holmes Collection came from a couple who resided in or near Hancock County, where they had attended one of our Greenfield tours. Charles W. Miller practiced law in Greenfield and Hancock County for many years.

Also found within the collection are Victorian Era calling cards with the surname Miller affixed. Ornate

Ornate Victorian Calling Cards. Size varies.

The Mystery of the H. H. Holmes Collection

cards bearing the names "Matilda B. Miller", "Mr. Frank Miller", Lizzie and C.F. Jones and several members of the "Zuekle" family can be found among the artifacts in the Holmes collection. These 19 cards are colorful and ornate and each features a name hidden under a flourished diecut flap. They are very similar in design and they are very Victorian. It is easy to imagine them being passed around between party guests as a formal introduction. Some surnames appear in pairs and trios, obviously from the same family.

One name stands out among them: Minnie Reitz. Miss Wilhelmine "Minnie" Reitz (1853-1926) was one of the seven sisters. Minnie was honored with a prestigious and exclusive appointment to the Board of Lady Managers of the 1893 Chicago World's Fair. She died, unmarried, at the Reitz Home at age 72. Were these cards mementos of a party held during the 1893 Fair? What's more, if these cards belonged to Dr. Holmes, why did he save them? When he carefully perused them, did he see the names of friends? Or prospective victims?

Was this macabre collection of relics and artifacts left with Judge Miller for safekeeping during one of Holmes's many trips to the Hoosier state before 1894? Were they evidence for prosecution, defense, or of complicity retained by a friend for a friend? Most likely, we'll never know. As for me, my money is on Charles W. Miller, the last victim of the curse of H. H. Holmes.

Detective David S. Richards

Knowing that the Holmes Collection has some connection to Indiana, the possibility exists that it was gathered for evidence in Indianapolis for a trial that never took place. Perhaps the items were gathered at the Irvington cottage murder site, or the hotel on the Circle, where the criminal stashed the Pitezel girls? Is it possible that it originated with a local investigator or policeman? If so, David S. Richards would be a worthy candidate.

During the summer of 1895, Holmes was being chased by Pinkerton Detective Agent Frank Geyer and an Indianapolis police officer, David S. Richards. Richards was first appointed to the Indianapolis Police Department in 1872. The Metropolitan Police Force was reorganized on April 14, 1883 into a new police force totaling 59 men. David S. Richards was a charter member of that first Indianapolis Police Department.

The Mystery of the H. H. Holmes Collection

When Detective Geyer arrived at Indianapolis Police Department headquarters on July 25, 1895, he asked for a member of the detective squad to assist in his search. Detective Richards, a 23-year veteran of the department and local legend, was assigned to assist him.

Richards was a local legend, who was once nearly killed in a gun battle with the murderous Modoc gang, who terrorized Indianapolis during the 1870's, committing over 200 robberies. The gang hid out in the "bottoms" area of Fall Creek near the Tennessee Street bridge, site of the original St. Vincent's Hospital and now home to Ivy Tech Community College.

At 10 a.m. on the morning of July 2, 1879, patrolmen David S. Richards and Jeptha W. Bradley came upon the suspects in the Fall Creek bottoms area. Almost immediately, patrolman Bradley was clubbed unconscious with a heavy object. At least 20 shots were fired during a brief but frantic gunfight. Richards was shot in the melee, but not before he returned fire, hitting gang member James "Jack" Carrigan in the head and left shoulder. The "Modoc" gang carried off their wounded compadre through the rain swollen waters of the White River at Cold Springs, not far from the present-day site of the Indianapolis Museum of Art.

The two wounded officers were taken to the Surgical Institute and word of their injuries quickly reached police headquarters. Richards had taken a bullet to the top of his head and his face was covered in blood. For a moment, his wounds were thought to be mortal, and in the frenzied first moments after he was discovered, Richards was reported as dead-on-arrival to the local newspapers. A physician took a closer look and discovered the officer

The Mystery of the H. H. Holmes Collection

was still very much alive. After regaining consciousness, it was discovered that Richards was shot three times: one bullet lodging in his left foot, another shearing off his left ear lobe and the third creasing his scalp. It was later determined that an additional four bullets had passed through his uniform coat missing him completely.

According to newspaper accounts of the day, when Chief of Police Al Travis arrived at the wounded officer's bedside, Richards stuck his hand out and said, "Chief, I'd a got my man if it hadn't been for 'Modoc' shooting me."

Indianapolis Police tracked 'Modoc' to Marseilles, Illinois, west of Chicago. They captured him on August 7, 1879 and charged him with shooting Patrolman Richards. On September 24, 1879, the jury found 'Modoc' guilty, fined him $50 and sentenced him to six months in the county jail for "assault and battery with intent to get away". Amazingly, 'Modoc' was pardoned before the 6 months was served out.

The wounds Richards received in that gun fight plagued him the rest of his life. Despite the severity of his injuries, Patrolman Richards returned to duty in November 1879.

Richards had been elevated to the post of detective by the time he was assigned to assist Pinkerton agent Geyer in the hunt for H. H. Holmes. The two detectives began their search by visiting every real estate office in and around Indianapolis over the course of several weeks, to no avail. On the evening of August 26th, while sitting in the lobby of their hotel, Geyer asked Richards if there were any small towns outside of Indianapolis they had yet to check.

The Mystery of the H. H. Holmes Collection

Richards responded, "Well, there's two, yet we haven't investigated, Irvington and Maywood." The detectives traveled to Irvington the next day.

Detective Sergeant David S. Richards retired from IPD in January of 1912 after 39 years and nine months of exemplary service. He was just four months shy of putting an 8th five-year stripe on his uniform, something no other officer had ever done, but the pain of his injuries suffered thirty-three years before deprived him of that singular honor. He had served more years on the department than any other man at that time. By now, the rumors of a curse upon all those involved in the Holmes crime and prosecution were well known and often the subject of follow-up newspaper columns.

After another member of the Holmes' jury committed suicide in March of 1912, The Indianapolis News contacted Detective Richards for comment about the Holmes' curse. Richards, now retired, had become somewhat of a legend in the city for the role he played in solving the murder of little Howard Pitezel. When asked about the curse, he told the reporter "I have to laugh at that story every time I hear it."

Despite laughing at the idea of a Holmes curse, Detective Richards began to experience searing pain in his left foot shortly after that interview. Richards, a tough old bird, understated the pain by telling friends, "it's just a twinge now and then." Richards finally visited the hospital on New Year's Day of 1922, seeking relief from the agony of his festering, open wound. There, doctors amputated his gangrenous foot caused by that unhealed bullet wound suffered forty-three years earlier. Two days later, on January 3, 1922, he passed away at Eastman hos- pital

The Mystery of the H. H. Holmes Collection

(a stone's throw from where Lucas Oil Stadium stands today) at the age of 75. Had the curse of H. H. Holmes struck again?

    As one of the detectives involved tracking down Holmes' visits to Indianapolis and Irvington, was it Richards who retained these relics of a murderer in the face of a curse he refused to believe, but ultimately fell victim to himself? Did he save them to show his family and reminisce about the good old days? Most likely, we'll never know the answer to that question. However, one thing remains clear, Detective David S. Richards' connection to the Holmes case in Indiana is unquestioned, his service to our state invaluable and has personal sacrifice undeniable.

Pat Quinlan

Pat Quinlan

Aside from this collection of mysterious relics and souvenirs, H. H. Holmes left behind his massive building at 63rd and Wallace in Chicago that the press dubbed "The Murder Castle." Here, it is believed, Holmes tortured and killed as many as two hundred victims, as systematically as cattle in a stockyard. The 3-story building was a maze of hallways with blind corners, doors that opened to brick walls and rooms that were escape-proof, with the only exit for guests being a greased chute leading to the basement.

The building was described in a contemporary newspaper article: "The castle was built admirably for a murder shop. A dumb waiter ran from the third floor to the basement and there were no connections with the dumb

The Mystery of the H. H. Holmes Collection

waiter on the intervening floors. The conveyance was big enough to admit a man riding upon it. On the top floor in one of the rooms was a gigantic stove. It was eight feet high and three feet in diameter. It was an ideal stove for the burning of a human body. A person could be thrown into the stove bodily and could be burned to nothing. In the basement were quicklime vats. Bodies could be thrown in quicklime and consumed."

Patrick Quinlan was hired by Holmes to be the caretaker of that "Murder Castle." Police described Quinlan as being "five feet, eight or nine inches tall, slim build with light curly hair, sandy mustache around 38-years-old" at the time. "Pat" Quinlan had done a good job portraying his innocence in the deeds that went on at the "Murder Castle". He said he was only an employee of H. H. Holmes, merely the janitor and nothing more. Although he admitted that he had helped build the secret trap doors and lined the killing rooms with asbestos to deaden the sound, Quinlan insisted that he knew nothing of their purpose, and had no part in the devilish machinations of his boss.

Quinlan claimed that he was only an ordinary employee who did what he was told unhesitatingly. Quinlan never questioned the authority of his boss, H. H. Holmes. He never asked who the many women were Holmes had visiting him. He never questioned why he would see them come in but never see them go out. He never asked where they went when they disappeared. He was an ideal servant. That was the face Pat Quinlan showed to the authorities and the role he played for the public, but the truth was vastly different. Pat Quinlan was playing games of his own in the "Murder Castle".

The Mystery of the H. H. Holmes Collection

Seems that the married Quinlan liked the ladies as much as his boss did. In 1893, he got a "Murder Castle" chambermaid named Lizzie pregnant. Pat's wife lived in Ohio, but would soon be joining her husband at the Castle in time to see the 1893 World's Fair. As the time for his wife's arrival drew ever nearer, heated arguments between Pat and his very pregnant mistress made Holmes aware of the problem. Quinlan asked his boss, Dr. Holmes, if he could deliver the baby and "keep it quiet so the missus don't find out." Quinlan's agitation grew as Holmes paused for a long uncomfortable minute before answering, "I'll do anything I can Pat."

The plan to deliver the baby changed days after his revelation to Dr. Holmes. Now Lizzie threatened to tell Pat's wife of their elicit love affair. Worse, Lizzie had already told her sister. Quinlan went to Holmes and explained the situation. Quinlan lured both his wife and sister-in-law to a small room in the "Murder Castle." He left the two women and met Holmes in the basement where the doctor turned on the open gas jets, filling the room with the deadly invisible killing atmosphere. Within a few minutes the two women were dead. Their bodies disposed of in the usual manner, and without a trace. Quinlan's problem was instantly solved and his silent loyalty was guaranteed forever.

Since Quinlan did an admirable job of keeping his mouth shut while proclaiming his innocence, no one will ever know what part he played in the murders at the Castle. What can be surmised is that Quinlan likely remained quiet for no other reason than fear of Dr. H. H. Holmes. One of the requirements of employment with Holmes was a life insurance policy for $5,000 naming Holmes as beneficiary. Quinlan also knew that the caretaker before him, a

The Mystery of the H. H. Holmes Collection

man named Robert Latimer, tried to blackmail Holmes after learning of the insurance scams. Pat's fellow employees told him Latimer simply disappeared one day.

During his trial in Philadelphia, Holmes said this of Latimer, his 13th victim: "Robert Latimer, a man who had for some years been in my employ as janitor, was my next victim. Several years previous, before I had ever taken human life, he had known of certain insurance work I had engaged in, and when, in after years, he sought to extort money from me, his own death and the sale of his body was the recompense meted out to him. I confined him within the secret room and slowly starved him to death. Of this room and its secret gas supply and muffled windows and doors, sufficient has already been printed.

Finally, needing its use for another purpose and because his pleadings had become almost unbearable, I ended his life. The partial excavation in the walls of this room found by the police was caused by Latimer's endeavoring to escape by tearing away the solid brick and mortar with his unaided fingers."

In September of 1893, one month before the Chicago World's Fair concluded, the "Murder Castle" caught fire in several different locations simultaneously. True to form, Holmes had insured the building with several companies for a total of $25,000 (equal to $657,000 in today's money). Investigators discovered strong evidence of a liquid accelerant used to start the blaze. The fire had not spread to the lower floors and the insurance company never paid Holmes's claim. The fire destroyed the top floor, but Holmes was never charged with arson. This fire, however, was the beginning of the end for H. H. Holmes.

H. H. Holmes paid for his misdeeds with death by hanging on May 7, 1896. But his former caretaker / janitor

The Mystery of the H. H. Holmes Collection

"Pat" Quinlan never escaped his own self-made prison. When the "Murder Castle" caught fire in September of 1893, he was arrested with Holmes but eventually freed. Quinlan was accused of starting the fire (which he most likely did), but it was his actions after the fire that tipped off Chicago Police that there may have been something more going on in that building than a botched attempted arson.

During the fire, many bones were found around Holmes's Castle. Holmes explained they were beef bones leftover from a time when the flat had been used as a restaurant during the World's Fair. He explained that the huge dumb waiter was used to convey those many pounds of beef. He explained that the asbestos was to make the house fireproof, and for insulation. H. H. Holmes had an answer for everything.

After the fire, Quinlan took several cartloads of garbage out of the "factory." The police searched the dumpster a week later, and found it mostly empty but found traces of obvious human ashes and bone fragments inside. In 1893, forensic science was still a long way away, and the discovery of a blood-soaked rag in the basement of the castle, could set off a plausible legal argument over whether it was blood or paint. A piece of bone was hard to differentiate between human or animal. Ironically, the first use of bone fragments as evidence would happen a few years later in 1897, just blocks from the "Murder Castle". Adolph Louis Luetgert (namesake of the A.L. Luetgert Sausage & Packing Company) was charged with murdering his wife and dissolving her body in lye in one of his factory's sausage vats. A bit of jaw bone found in the factory (which was thriving at the same time as the "Murder Castle") was identified as the remains of

The Mystery of the H. H. Holmes Collection

Adolph's wife, Louisa.

The fire didn't level the building, as some accounts say, but it did destroy a lot of evidence. Quinlan, along with his wife, continued to live in the burned out shell of the old "Murder Castle" while Holmes was on trial. But the reputation of the place as the local haunted house was drawing negative attention from the Chicago press. Meantime, many reporters, vandals and curious gawkers broke into the Castle, wandering its maze-like corridors, staring at its grotesqueries, stealing Holmes' abandoned belongings, and generally destroying it as a crime scene. The vandals drove Pat Quinlan out of the "Murder Castle" for good.

On August 2, 1895, after Holmes was locked up securely in Philadelphia's Moyamensing Prison, Patrick Quinlan (and ironically his wife) turned state's evidence and testified against his former boss. Quinlan, now comfortable that he was out of Holmes' reach, described his former boss to police detectives as a "dirty, lying scoundrel" who should be hung for his crimes and that "he (Quinlan) would only be too willing to spring the trap."

The Mystery of the H. H. Holmes Collection

Quinlan testified at Holmes's trial that he was aware of the practice of stealing bodies from Western Michigan graveyards under the direction of Holmes. These bodies were then sold to local college and university medical schools, no questions asked. Quinlan's wife testified to this, too. Both claimed they were aware of the practice, but did not participate in the actual grave robberies. It was reported Quinlan and another man only received the bodies and participated in the "remaking and lining" of coffins for corpses before sale for medical use.

While he remained in Chicago, Quinlan claimed that the Castle was haunted by Holmes' many victims. He told friends that his former employer would visit him in his sleep, that the victims roamed the halls and pecked on the windows of the Castle. That the spirits followed him even after he moved back to a farmhouse in his Portland, Michigan hometown. By the spring of 1914, Pat Quinlan was a broken man.

When the Quinlan's went back to his home state of Michigan, he found himself the center of suspicious eyes and backhanded whispers. Everywhere he went, he was stared at and treated as fodder for gossip. While the rest of the world forgot Holmes, the little town where Quinlan lived continued to speculate about how much he really knew. His closest friends said that Pat Quinlan often reproached himself for his part in the dastardly affair. He told friends and family that he blamed himself for not suspecting Holmes and turning him in to the police. He was clearly dealing with demons all his own many years after his ex-employer was dead.

For nineteen years Quinlan was unable to sleep peacefully because of the awful experiences he endured during his employment by Holmes and the period immediately after. He would wake up at night screaming and cov-

The Mystery of the H. H. Holmes Collection

ered with sweat. He experienced these night terrors almost every night; calling for help and when a light would be brought to his room or when the electric switch would be turned on, he would recount how he was "attacked while half asleep by strange hallucinations".

On March 7, the former caretaker of the "Murder Castle", scribbled a note reading, "I could not sleep." He then committed suicide by drinking from a bottle of pesticide whose active ingredient was strychnine. Pat's facial muscles stretched tight and a peculiar metallic taste flooded his mouth. His calf muscles began to stiffen and convulse, his toes curled up under his feet and as his head thrashed back-and-forth, with blinding flashes of light darting across his eyes. His body went ice cold as he drifted off into that final sleep. Witnesses claimed that in death, he looked as though he had been carried there by the ghosts of the slain women of the Castle he once helped build. Pat Quinlan's death did not cause much of a stir. His name would be forgotten, but as you might expect, his death was immediately connected to the curse of H. H. Holmes.

Quinlan's connection to the Holmes Collection rests solely on the fact that there are two photos in the collection that have been identified as being Pat Quinlan.

One is a cabinet photo from the studio of Phillips & Bergstresser of Danville, Illinois, a town 140 miles due south of Chicago, on the route to Indianapolis. The cabinet photo depicts a man in the prime life with a chiseled, hardened look and a thick, bushy mustache.

The other photo is much smaller, with Pat Quinlan's name written in pencil on back. The rich sepia-toned photo resembles a modern-day passport photo. The differ-

The Mystery of the H. H. Holmes Collection

Cabinet photo of Pat Quinlan from the studio of Phillips & Bergstresser, Danville, IL. 6½" x 4¼" From the Holmes Collection.

Photograph of Pat Quinlan. Signed on the back. 1¾" x 1¼" From the Holmes Collection.

Newspaper sketches of Pat Quinlan, drawn during the trial of H.H. Holmes.

145

The Mystery of the H. H. Holmes Collection

ence is that this time, the man is wearing eyeglasses, his heavily combed hair is parted in the middle and held down with generous amounts of pomade. This smaller photo appears to be the same man but this image appears to be an attempt to alter, or disguise his appearance.

These photos represent the only known photographs of "Murder Castle" caretaker Pats Quinlan. Most of what we know about the enigmatic Quinlan comes from court transcripts, police interviews and newspaper stories written or gathered at the time of the crime. The most famous story, recounted earlier in this section, comes from a newspaper article titled "Hounded To Death By Ghosts Of The Castle He Built". The story appeared in **The Ogden Standard** newspaper on July 4, 1914 four months after Quinlan's death. It featured an artist stylized image of H.H. Holmes alongside a real photo image of the Murder Castle and another real photo image of a man identified as Pat Quinlan. Since no other images of Quinlan existed, this man's image was accepted as that of the

The *Ogden Standard Newspaper* article about the death of Pat Quinlan kicked off the Curse of H.H. Holmes. In this article, Quinlan is supposed pictured in the center. The image at right shows the Irish labor leader Pat Quinlan in 1913.

The Mystery of the H. H. Holmes Collection

doomed caretaker.

While researching this volume, I uncovered evidence that the shoddy journalism that plagued the Holmes case during the Victorian Era continued well into the Progressive Era. While the photo does picture Pat Quinlan, it is not the right Pat Quinlan. The man pictured in the curse article is Patrick L. Quinlan, Irish-American trade union organizer, journalist and Socialist labor leader / activist. This Patrick Quinlan, born in 1883 while H. H. Holmes was a student at Michigan University, died of natural causes in 1948. A close comparison of the man in the curse article alongside an image of Patrick L. Quinlan reveals the error.

Did the Holmes Collection belong to Patrick Quinlan or one of his descendants? If so, what was the purpose of saving it? Knowing Quinlan's unsavory reputation and sad history, it is not hard to imagine that a conman like Pat Quinlan may well have sold the items for easy cash.

After all, Quinlan had unfettered access to the "Murder Castle" and all its contents for a decade after the crimes that made it infamous were committed. Since the family blamed Holmes for Pat's death, wouldn't they want the collection gone?

Georgiana Yoke

Before I start, I must confess that most of what I know about Georgiana Yoke I have learned from author Judith Nickels. While researching the items contained in the Holmes Collection during the filming of the *American Ripper* TV series in early 2017, I came across Ms. Nickels' excellent book: ***A Competent Witness. Georgiana Yoke and the Trial of H. H. Holmes***. Her book is the result of eight years of research by the author, during which time she literally retraced the steps of the book's main character.

Georgiana Yoke was born on October 17, 1869 in Clark County, Illinois. She grew up in Edinburgh, IN and graduated from Edinburgh high school in the spring of 1888. She continued her education at the Central Normal College in Danville, Indiana, a school of around 500 students. Central Normal College offered strong Christian-based co-educational opportunities. As with Butler College, then in Irvington, a young woman could obtain the same education as a man. Central Normal espoused revolutionary principles such as:

The Mystery of the H. H. Holmes Collection

- Study can be made more attractive than mischief;
- Individuality of the pupil is sacred;
- Co-education of the sexes is essential to intellectual development, good behavior and purity;
- A true teacher is always a friend and guide, never a boss or master."

After graduation, Georgiana taught school in Columbus, Indiana for a couple years before moving to Chicago in the summer of 1892. There, she moved in with her uncle, Isaac Toner (her mother's younger brother), and went to work as a sales clerk in the men's handkerchief department at the Siegel Cooper store at State, Van Buren and Congress Streets. It was here that Georgiana first encountered H. H. Holmes.

In March 1893 Holmes began his courtship of Georgiana and asked her to marry him later that summer. She accepted, and became the third and final wife of H. H. Holmes, on January 17, 1894, in Denver, Colorado. Holmes neglected to inform her that he was still married to both of his previous wives.

Most historians believe that Georgiana was oblivious to Holmes career as a murderer. She knew Holmes as a medical doctor, an entrepreneur, business man and inventor. She was anxious to take her new fiancé back home to Franklin, just south of Indianapolis, for a proper introduction to her mother. In the Fall of 1894, Georgiana got her chance.

The newly married couple very likely visited the Yoke family farmhouse in Indianapolis, just southeast of Garfield Park. Georgiana's paternal grandparents, Richardson Allen Yoke and his wife Isabelle, were important pioneers in Indianapolis history, and were among the founders

The Mystery of the H. H. Holmes Collection

of Garfield Park, located not far from Irvington. Their house, built in 1890 at a cost of $250, was a two-story plain white clapboard structure with two large rooms on each floor. The property also featured a smokehouse, poultry house, carriage house and two barns.

Georgiana also took her new husband to visit her mother, Mary, at her home located at 248 S. State Street in Franklin, Indiana. (Her father, John, had died in 1880). For the sake of propriety during their visit, Georgiana stayed in her mother's home while her husband stayed at a hotel near the college. Many believe that this is where Holmes plotted to murder both his new wife and her mother. Luckily, he never got the opportunity to commit this crime as he was arrested and jailed on November 17, 1894 for the murder of Benjamin Pitezel.

Years later, Mary Yoke's house was absorbed by Franklin College and demolished in the early 2000's. But her close brush with death made a fascinating story, which kept interest in Georgianna and Holmes alive. I visited Franklin, Indiana and the Johnson County museum for further research on the Yoke family. Archivist Linda Talley produced documents from these museum archives including priceless eyewitness accounts of Holmes and Georgiana on the streets of Franklin in the fall of 1894.

One letter, written by Myrtle Peggs of Anderson, Indiana in 1962, states:

> *"Some how I missed 'High Society' & was not acquainted with the Culprite [sic] (Culprit) in question. However I did have the honor (?) of seeing him once. I was going to town one day and when turned corner at Yandes & Jefferson streets going West, I saw Georgiana & a man approaching &*

The Mystery of the H. H. Holmes Collection

hearing a lot of rumors concerning them I took a good look at him. He had been seen by about everyone in Franklin. It was reported by everyone as wearing black suit, black silk hat & flourished a cane with large gold head. Looked like black broadcloth of rather unusual type rather long coat & was strutting along. I did not know Georgiana personaly [sic]. Was blonde & nice-looking. Was a puzzel [sic] to all the inhabitants in our small town. I heard gossip of the family leaving but as so far I don't know where."

Despite the work of multiple researchers, and years of painstaking research, no verifiable photograph of Georgiana Yoke is known to exist. Could any of the photos found within the Holmes Collection be that of the mysterious Miss Yoke?

There are a few images of Georgiana in the form of courtroom artist renderings and news accounts from the trial, but as you can see, none are very flattering or accurate. What we are left with are the personal descriptions of Georgiana's contemporaries and eyewitness accounts from newspapers. The newspaper drawings all show a woman with a long, narrow, straight nose, high cheekbones, and large, downcast eyes. She is drawn with a very small waist; her tight, high-necked, gigot-sleeve dress makes it impossible to tell if she was equally slender in the throat and shoulders. Her hair is variously called yellow, golden, and "decidedly blond."

She is described in typically Victorian era terminology. From ***The Philadelphia Inquirer***:

"... a most delicate build, a mere girl in size an appearance. Her beautiful oval face, with its del-

The Mystery of the H. H. Holmes Collection

icately-tinted cheeks, bore a look of terror, which the downcast eyes intensified. She was dressed in a neat-fitting and becoming gown of black, her stylishly-trimmed hat was of the same color, and her gloves harmonized with the rest of her somber attire."

The newspapers refer to her as a "girl" or a "child-bride," even though at the time of the trial she was twenty-six years old. However, most accounts were generally sympathetic to her plight.

One of the most remarkable descriptions of Georgiana appeared in the **Galveston Daily News** in July of 1895:

". . . Mrs. Pratt was a remarkably beautiful woman. All critics agree on that. It was one of those winning, attractive faces that you cannot get away from any more than you can believe the possessor capable of evil. It was a fresh and beautiful face, with the fine hopes and aspirations of youth in it and one that once seen remained an indelible memory. She wound her way unconsciously into the heart of every person who met her. She had that way about her which takes hold of the roots of things in an instant. She was as gentle and refined in manner and personal conduct as it was possible to be."

The article goes on to quote Judge Hunter, their landlord:

"Pratt's wife was one of the most beautiful women I ever met. She was just one of those women who can make you like them. She was a most winning person and everybody who came in contact with her acknowledged the spell of her presence. She would

The Mystery of the H. H. Holmes Collection

Three different newspaper sketches made of Georgiana Yoke during her testimony at her husband's trial.

> *make friends rapidly. She was not a woman of expensive tastes or distinguished manner. It was because she was simple and elegant that people felt drawn to her. She appeared to idolize her husband..."*

Much has been made of Georgiana's unusually big blue eyes, which one newspaper called "dreamy" and a neighbor called "so large as to be considered a defect." Judith Nickels makes the case in ***A Competent Witness***, that she suffered from ophthalmic goiter, which today would be diagnosed as Graves' disease. This condition, which causes the muscles of the eye to swell and push on the eyeball, can fluctuate, so it is possible that at times she looked quite normal, and at other times her eyes had a staring or startled quality. It is interesting that all the contemporary courtroom sketches show Georgiana with her eyes closed.

A 1962 account of Georgiana's appearance from Ethelyn Pedlow, who lived at 3038 Central Avenue in Indianapolis, can also be found in the files of the Johnson County library. Pedlow had been a neighbor of Georgiana for many years. The account states:

The Mystery of the H. H. Holmes Collection

"Mrs. Pedlow said that she and Georgiana had been what she called "porch acquaintances." They had not been close, but it was evident that Mrs. Pedlow had regarded her somewhat aloof neighbor with admiration. I wished to know how Georgiana had looked, what sort of person she had been, and so forth. Mrs. Pedlow replied with an emphatic and spontaneous compliment. Pitching her voice a little deeper in a way that conveyed approval, she exclaimed, "Handsome woman." She described Georgiana as dignified, courteous, well-dressed, and well-educated. She told us that she and several other neighbors had known of Georgiana's former notoriety, but that, nevertheless, whatever they may have expected, they had all come to regard Georgiana as a respectable and even exemplary lady."

Georgiana Yoke, although married to H.H. Holmes for less than a year, traveled extensively with her husband and was often entrusted with her husband's papers and possessions. Mr. and Mrs. Howard (aka Holmes) visited Indianapolis and Franklin during their travels through the Hoosier state. After Holmes was convicted and ultimately hanged for his crimes, Georgiana and her mother, Mary were effectively chased out of Franklin to the relative obscurity of big-city Indianapolis by her small-town gossipy neighbors.

Georgiana ultimately married a former Siegel – Cooper department store co-worker named Harry Chapman and moved to Santa Ana, California. She died on July 20, 1945 from a heart attack at the age of 75.

During her husband's trial, Georgiana Yoke testified against him in a Philadelphia courtroom on October

The Mystery of the H. H. Holmes Collection

31, 1895: Halloween. According to the trial transcript, Georgiana described a pair of diamond earrings as being among the gifts Holmes had given her.

A researcher from Franklin whose collection was donated to the Johnson County library many years ago, documented a 1999 phone call with members of the Yoke family, John and Micki Yoke. During that call, Micki revealed that a packet of Holmes associated items were sent to Georgiana's family in Syracuse, New York after Georgiana's death in 1945. The packet was sent by Georgiana's second husband, Harry Chapman, as instructed in her will. Among its contents was a pair of diamond earrings.

Judy Nickels relates, "When Georgiana died, she passed the pair of earrings on to her much younger sister-in-law. When the sister-in-law died, she divided the pair between her own daughter and daughter-in-law. The daughter had her diamond made into a ring, which has been lost. But the daughter-in-law kept hers in a box at the bank, and in the early 1990's, someone in the family happened to read Harold Schechter's book, **Depraved**. Only after reading that book did the family connect the fact that the Georgiana Yoke portrayed in it was their great aunt, and the single diamond earring in their bank box was a gift from H. H. Holmes. Nickels has a letter from the late Mary Yoke, the daughter-in-law who saved the earring, describing all this. Since she passed away a few years ago, Nickels assumed that the earring went to her daughter per the family tradition." Once again, we find a souvenir associated with H. H. Holmes. How hard would it to be to imagine that this collection of artifacts passed from generation to generation along with that diamond.

The possibility of Georgiana Yoke's ownership of

The Mystery of the H. H. Holmes Collection

the Holmes Collection is based on her close ties to Central Indiana and the question of whether one of these photos is that of the elusive Miss Yoke. However, there are additional plausible theories why she may have been the owner.

In August of 2017, Judy Nickels traveled from her Chicago home to visit the Bona Thompson Center in Irvington. Our hope was for her to look through the photos contained in the Holmes Collection to see if Georgiana's image may be found among them. There are a couple of photos that were identified as Georgiana by ***The American Ripper*** researchers. Judy looked at those photos and proclaimed that none of them were Georgiana.

I noticed that as she glanced through the images, she segregated two of the images from the group. One was of a little girl and the other a bespectacled older lady. She said the older lady stood out for her, but she couldn't say why.

It was the photo of the little girl that she focused on the most. The cabinet photo, taken at the Fearnaught photography studio at 16 E. Washington St. in Indianapolis, pictures a beautiful young girl with light colored hair and big eyes in a stylish dress featuring lace

Cabinet card photo of a young girl, possibly of a Young Georgiana Yoke.

The Mystery of the H. H. Holmes Collection

cuffs and an intricate lace bodice.

The more Judy held the photo, the more she thought, "This could be Georgiana." As for the older lady, Judy said she just "had a feeling" about that image. During our meeting, Judy also shared a story about Holmes the souvenir collector. "You know, Holmes left several trunks full of stuff in storage at Georgiana's mother's house in Franklin." She said. "No one knew what was in the trunks or what became of them but the family talked about those trunks for years."

Judy, never one to miss an opportunity to walk in the footsteps of her muse, scheduled a trip to the Yoke family farmhouse to speak with some family descendants. The following day, I received a call from Judy from the farmhouse, in which she said, "Do you remember that photo of the older lady?" I answered, "Yes, I do." She continued, "Well, I'm holding a photo of that same woman in my hands right now! You need to see this. Here, let me get Chris." Within seconds I was talking to the homeowner, Chris Yoke, arranging a trip out to the farmhouse the next day.

I traveled out to Shelby County, just outside the Marion County line, to visit the Yoke family. It was my good fortune to find out that Chris, Georgiana Yoke's second cousin three times removed, is an accomplished genealogist and Yoke family historian.

Chris informed me that the farmhouse sits on the original 1841 Yoke family land and that his house, built in 1876, was the Yoke family gathering place for generations. Today, the home is a shrine-like museum to the Yoke & Moore families. Chris and I studied the photos in the Holmes collection hoping that we might find a family

The Mystery of the H. H. Holmes Collection

connection. Although Chris and his wife Vicky studied the images carefully, even singling out a few to compare to family pictures hanging on the walls, Chris quietly and confidently said, "I don't see my family here." Although I had hoped to find a connection to the Yokes, I trusted Chris's assessment.

I singled out the two photos that Judy had lingered on the previous day and Chris compared the photo of the older lady and said, "Close, but no cigar." When we focused on the photo of the little girl, Chris admitted that it could be Georgiana but who knows? Without another image to compare it to, it remains an impossible task. Judy Nickels is up to that task and at the time of this writing, she is working hard to find more answers about that photo.

A few days later, I received an e-mail from Judy, she had done her homework. "Fearnaught (the photographer) was established in Indianapolis in 1872. If it is Georgiana, it was probably taken around 1874-76, when she was between 5 and 7 years old. The hairstyle and sash on the back of the dress are consistent with 1870's styles, and the quality of the photograph certainly looks like others from the time. And that kid's eyes are definitely blue." Keep in mind Judy has been researching Georgiana for a decade now so if she says there's a chance, then there's a chance.

Even though Chris Yoke was not able to make the connection, he did share with me a postcard from Georgiana and a visitor's book to the farmhouse, both with Georgiana's signatures on them. He also admitted that he was intrigued at the idea and had developed a theory. He believed that if this collection did belong to Georgiana,

The Mystery of the H. H. Holmes Collection

Postcard written by Georgiana Yoke. Dated August 18, 1910.

Holmes may have been gathering photos for use in a future insurance fraud case. I asked the couple if they believed that Holmes, had he not been caught in Philadelphia, was planning to kill Georgiana and her mother to file yet another false claim.

Vicky Yoke answered, "Well, Holmes had bought her all that expensive jewelry and was planning on taking her and her mother to Germany. That was like a mobile bank account. He could have cashed in that necklace and earrings and never looked back." The mystery of the Holmes collection continues.

Benjamin Pitezel

Benjamin Freelon Pitezel was born in Henry County, Illinois on May 19, 1856. He was an itinerate carpenter who joined Holmes's in the construction of the "Murder Castle" in November of 1889. Because Pitezel was an alcoholic, small-time con man, Holmes quickly deduced that he could control him. Benjamin was one of the few people whom Holmes actually confided in. Pitezel married Carrie Canning of Galva, Illinois in 1877. Together, they became parents to six children. Pitezel does all sorts of things for Holmes, on both sides of the law, but the extent of what he knew about Holmes's murders is unclear.

Pitezel became a household name during the nationwide search for his three missing children. Holmes's run in Chicago was over, and he quickly came up with a new scheme to make money. Holmes instructed Carrie Pitezel to take out a $10,000 life insurance policy on her husband, with Holmes as beneficiary. He would then have Benjamin drink

The Mystery of the H. H. Holmes Collection

a cocktail of Holmes's own creation that would render him unconscious, after which a local doctor would be summoned to declare Ben dead. Holmes plan was to "doctor" up Ben's face to make it look as though her husband had died in a fire. When the doctor left to call an ambulance, a corpse would be substituted for Ben's body, and the insurance company would declare the heavily insured man had died of injuries sustained in the fire.

Pitezel moved to Philadelphia in the early Fall of 1894 and rented an office space at 1316 Callowhill Street. He hung out a sign declaring his business as "Patents Bought and Sold. B.F. Perry". Holmes arranged for the "accident" to take place on September 4, 1894. Although neighbors later said they had heard a loud explosion on that day, oddly, nobody called the authorities to investigate the source. The next morning, a carpenter named Eugene Smith, visited the office, but found the door locked and the blinds drawn.

Sensing something was wrong, Smith summoned a nearby policeman and together they forced their way into the office. There they found the badly burnt body of a man lying face down in the back of the office, an empty bottle of Benzine, a pipe and several spent wooden matchsticks were found scattered near the body. The death was declared an accident and the body was sent to the morgue. There it remained for eleven days as an unclaimed John Doe. Eventually it was buried in an unmarked plot in the Philadelphia potter's field.

Carrie filed an insurance claim stating that B.F. Perry was really her husband, the none-too-bright Benjamin Pitezel. She believed that her husband was safe and sound with her three children hiding out somewhere safe from harm. She had no idea just how mistaken she was.

The Mystery of the H. H. Holmes Collection

Carrie didn't know that after Holmes got her husband hopelessly drunk, he killed Ben Pitezel while he was passed out on the floor. Ironically, Holmes was convicted and executed for just one single murder: that of Benjamin Pitezel.

At first, in Holmes's Own Story, he maintained that Pitezel's death was suicide. The suicide note, which, naturally Holmes had to destroy, asked him to stage the death as part of a crime scene. "He wished me to so arrange his body in one of two ways that it would appear that his death had been either accidental or that he had been attacked by burglars and killed, giving the details of how I was to carry our either course: First, that his family should not at present know of his death; second, that the children should never know he had committed suicide..."

Later, while Holmes languished in prison trying to save his own skin, the doctor reflected on his rela- tionship with his carpenter cohort. "Benjamin F. Pitezel ... It will be understood that from the first hour of our acquaintance, even before I knew he had a family who would later afford me additional victims for the gratification of my blood-thirstiness, I intended to kill him..." Holmes stated.

Holmes continues, "Only one difficulty presented itself. It was necessary, for me to kill him in such a manner that no struggle or movement of his body should occur, otherwise his clothing being in any way displaced it would have been impossible to again put them in a normal condition. I overcame this difficulty by first binding him hand and foot and having done — I proceeded to burn him alive by saturating his clothing and his face with benzene and igniting it with a match."

Along the way, Holmes came up with several ex-

The Mystery of the H. H. Holmes Collection

planations on the method he used to kill Ben Pitezel. He claimed that he used chloroform to knock Ben out and then burnt his former friend's face with an acetylene torch.

A few accounts claim that Holmes delighted in torturing the man with the torch while Ben was still alive. Holmes also claimed that he fed embalming fluid to Pitezel through the alcohol Ben was copiously consuming on the day of his death.

Newspaper sketch of the murder of Benjamin Pitezel.

Holmes couldn't bring Carrie to Philadelphia to identify the body knowing she would see who it really was. Holmes presented himself as a virtual uncle to the children, and convinced Carrie to allow three of her children to travel with him. So, Holmes brought fourteen-year-old Alice to Philadelphia to identify her father's body. On September 20th, she wrote to her mother: "Just arrived Philadelphia this morning ... I am going to the Morgue after awhile ... Have you gotten 4 letters from me besides this?" Holmes intercepted and never mailed any of her letters, stashing them in a tin box.

The most compelling reason that the Holmes Collection may have been assembled by, or connected to the doomed Benjamin Pitezel rests in a single photo found within. It is a 2½" wide by 3¾" tall cabinet photo with no photo studio name or any other identifying marks on it.

The Mystery of the H. H. Holmes Collection

When the collection was presented to the researchers working on the H. H. Holmes *American Ripper* documentary, they singled the image out as none other than Benjamin Freelon Pitezel himself. A contemporary description of Ben said this: "Pitezel was well over six-feet tall, weighed nearly 14 stone (nearly 200 lbs.), had thick dark hair and sported a trim moustache on a once handsome face now worn by the ravages of alcohol."

Pitezel may be the saddest of all possible collection owners presented here. He is remembered more for the way he died than for the way he lived. The feckless, alcoholic carpenter probably never knew what hit him. While he had a history of arrests ranging from barroom brawls, theft and fraud to horse stealing, his chief crime may have been that he fell under the hypnotic control of America's first serial killer. One such brawl in November of 1889, reportedly while acting as muscle for his boss, cost Pitezel a broken nose and the loss of his two front teeth. Judging by the vigorous image purported to be Ben Pitezel found within this collection, it was taken some time in the mid-1880s.

Ben wasn't even allowed to rest in peace. The September 4, 1895 issue of the *Trenton Evening Times* newspaper in New Jersey reported on the un-

Newspaper sketch of Benjamin Pitezel.

Cabinet card photograph of Benjamin Pitezel.

Cabinet card photograph believed to be of Benjamin Pitezel.

The Mystery of the H. H. Holmes Collection

quiet repose of Pitezel, one year to the day of his death in a news item titled "Pitezel's Body Again Exhumed"

"The decapitated body of B. F. Pitzel [sic], one of the supposed victims of H. H. Holmes, was again exhumed from the American Mechanics' cemetery by the coroner's physicians. The coffin, with its ghastly burden, was carried into the toolshed of the cemetery, but the utmost vigilance was maintained to keep the object of the exhumation a secret. It was subsequently learned that one of the bones of the leg had been removed and the body reinterred."

Aside from his family, poor Ben Pitezel never really had anything of his own. He lived a sad, alcohol fueled existence for the last decade of his life. His home, tools, food and whiskey money all came from H. H. Holmes. Although in my opinion, his ownership of the Holmes Collection is unlikely, it is not entirely implausible. In Ben Pitezel's case, having something may have been better than nothing at all.

Emeline Cigrand

Emeline Cigrand

One of Holmes's victims, Emeline Cigrand, was a beautiful 20-something stenographer from Lafayette, Indiana, whose skeleton Holmes reportedly sold to Chicago's Rush Medical College. Emeline was originally from Anderson, Indiana, and her family still resided there at the time of her disappearance and death.

Emeline had worked with alcoholics at the Keeley Institute in Dwight, Illinois while Ben Pitezel was drying out there. Her experience made her a good candidate for employment at Holmes's bogus Silver Ash Institute in northern New York State. In the May 17, 1893 issue of the Northern Tribune from Gouverneur, NY, an advertisement appeared reading:

The Mystery of the H. H. Holmes Collection

"Drunkenness Cured! Northern New York Silver Ash Institute. For the Cure of Morphine, Alcohol and Opium Habits! A Cure Guaranteed in Every Case or No Pay! No. 10 State Street Watertown N.Y.

J. W. Holmes Pres't."

Emeline took a job as a stenographer in Chicago, but soon asked to return to her Anderson, Indiana home to marry her longtime boyfriend, Robert Phelps. When Holmes refused to grant her request, Phelps came to Chicago to retrieve her. After Phelps walked into the castle, neither he nor Emeline were ever seen again. Holmes wrote to her parents with a story claiming that their daughter had eloped with Mr. Phelps. Holmes went so far as to have wedding invitations printed for the doomed couple, but the invitations gave no addresses for the ceremony.

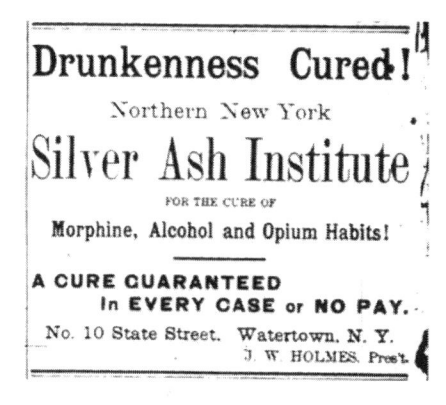

Related to the story of Emeline's disappearance, there's the story of Myron George "M.G." Chappell, a skeleton "articulator" to whom Holmes is said to have sold fresh bodies to be made into skeletons. Chappell was born in Chicago around 1850. He is listed in various census reports and records as a laborer, painter, private detective, railroad engineer, and stationary engineer. In other words, Chappel was a handy man to have around for H. H.

167

The Mystery of the H. H. Holmes Collection

Holmes.

In 1895, Chappell told police that he had answered an advertisement around the July 4, 1893, placed by a man named Harry Gordon (alias H. H. Holmes). The ad sought someone to articulate three dead bodies. He claimed that he obtained the bodies, along with a trunk, from Holmes at 53rd and Wallace, in the Inglewood section of South Chicago. Chappell said the bodies were of one man and two women. One of the bodies was later alleged to be that of Emeline Cigrand.

Chappell claimed that he had sold two of the skeletons, on Holmes behalf, to local medical schools. "But what became of the third body," the police asked? Chappell claimed he still had it. Well, at least a part of it. Chappell told police the skull, painted red, was hanging from a tree in his yard, and there was also a stocking full of hair in a trunk.

Chappell took the police to his house and cut the skull down from his tree. He then gave them an old Saratoga trunk containing a half-articulated skeleton and a stocking full of hair, as well as some books on anatomy and articulation. At the Castle, he showed them a room where he'd been given the bodies and the spot in the basement were Holmes had kept an acid vat, among other things. Here, he told them, Holmes had boiled down the greater part of the victim's body before giving them to him and a man named Richardson to articulate and sell to colleges. He went on to say that Holmes and Richardson then began to bring many more bodies to his house.

According to the July 31, 1895 issue of the ***Carroll (Iowa) Herald*** newspaper, Chappell told police,

The Mystery of the H. H. Holmes Collection

"I was given the body of the female with the flesh of the face torn off. The body of the woman was stretched out there against the west wall (of the Chicago Murder Castle). It was so disfigured that identification would be impossible. The skin on the face was cut around and then torn back like a mask over the forehead. The flesh was also hacked to an inch above the roots of the hair. The body and limbs were not mutilated. I cut the arms off and carried them home, Holmes brought the trunk and lower limbs to me, also quartered, after nightfall...

Holmes made a great to-do before me as to how he supplied the college boys with cadavers and full-rigged skeletons at cut rate. That was why I asked no questions, as I was not an expert I was glad for his trade to learn the business. Holmes had two acid vats in the basement where he got rid of flesh and bleached bones."

Chappell's explanation for hanging onto that last body? He was never paid for his work. Chapman kept the young Miss Cigrand's skeleton after realizing he'd been stiffed. The skull he turned over to Chicago Police Inspector John Fitzpatrick belonged to Emeline. The police believed the other bodies were Anna Williams, the sister of one of Holmes's wives, and Emeline's doomed fiancé, Robert E. Phelps.

Most of the places Chappell told investigators to dig turned up nothing, but they did find a metal tank in the space where he said the acid pit was located. Inside contained some crude petroleum, but nothing to indicate that it had ever been used to bleach bones. None of the other vats Chappell told police about were ever found.

The Mystery of the H. H. Holmes Collection

Many fantastical details of Chappell's story were completely dismissed. It didn't help that his son, Charles, and his wife, Cynthia, both told police that M.G. was a drunkard and inveterate liar. They claimed that Chappell would make up wild stories when he was drinking, and then he'd forget what he'd said after he sobered up. The trunk, they claimed, had belonged to Chappell's mother, who was now in a Home for Incurables, and the hair in the stocking was hers. Most reporters noted that Chappell was drunk whenever he showed up at the Castle for interviews.

Furthermore, none of the residents, shop keepers or employees, who lived and worked in the Castle, recognized him. While Chappell did tell wild stories, he seemed to have inside information about Holmes. "Chappell may be a little confused on his dates, but when he can take us, as he has, to Holmes' house and say 'dig there and you will find so and so,' and we dig and find what he says. I take it to mean that Chappell knows what he is talking about." said Chicago Police Chief John J. Badenoch. However, his stories about the bones coming from the Holmes "Castle" were difficult to verify, and easy to refute.

In those days there was no way to tell whose body a skeleton had been, or even exactly how old the skeleton was. There was no DNA testing available to see if the hair really belonged to Granny Chappell, or if the skeleton matched Emeline Cigrand. Police kept the bones in storage for years, and they were displayed to a jury a few years later when Patrick Quinlan, Holmes' janitor, tried to sue the police. Chappell promised police that he could furnish photographs and pictures from the "Castle" that would prove who worked there. True to his word, Chappell came back to the station later with photographs that he claimed came from the "Castle", including a group

The Mystery of the H. H. Holmes Collection

photo, but none of them proved to be pertinent to their investigation, which had by now switched to Philadelphia.

Myron George Chappell died in 1929, and is buried in Chicago's Mt. Greenwood Cemetery.

Could the Holmes Collection belong to Chappell? Or to the doomed Emeline Cigrand? Could their images be found hidden among these photos? And what happened to those photos Chappell brought to police in 1895? Several newspapers reported on the story, but none seem to have published any of the photos, or even furnished good descriptions of them.

Frank P Geyer

Pinkerton Detective Frank P. Geyer

The hero of the Holmes saga was a Pinkerton detective agency operative named Frank P. Geyer. Geyer, a carpenter by trade before becoming a Philadelphia policeman, knew better than most the traps and pitfalls of H.H. Holmes' murderous legacy. It was Geyer who chased Holmes all over the Midwest and Canada after Holmes's misdeeds had been discovered within the walls of his Chicago hotel.

Geyer made several trips to Indianapolis in search of Holmes, who was known to have had marital family located here. On his last trip, Geyer was looking not for Holmes, but rather for the children of his business partner, Benjamin Pitezel. As a part of an insurance swindle cooked up by the two men, Holmes was traveling with three of Pitezel's children, Alice, Nellie and Howard.

The Mystery of the H. H. Holmes Collection

Perhaps the best evidence from that awful Irvington visit can be found in the memoir written by Pinkerton detective Frank Geyer. In his memoir, *The Holmes – Pitezel case. A history of the greatest crime of the century and the search for the missing Pitezel children*, Geyer stated,

> "I must confess that I returned to Indianapolis in no cheerful frame of mind...I believed the boy had been murdered in Indianapolis, or in some nearby town, but my ill success at locating the house, after so much effort and such wide publicity, greatly annoyed and puzzled me. The mystery seemed to be impenetrable. The desire on the part of the police authorities of Indianapolis to assist me in the search, never wavered. On this, ny third return to that city, I was greeted with the same kindness and unvarying courtesy I had enjoyed on the previous occasions."

Beginning on August 27, 1895, over 10 months after the boy's death, Detective Geyer and Mr. Gary, an investigator with the insurance company, took the trolley from Indianapolis to Irvington to search for the boy. Mr. Brown, a real estate agent in Irvington, identified the photo of Holmes and recalled renting a cottage to the man in question.

Detective Geyer was taken to the cottage but Holmes was long gone. He questioned homeowner's handymen, Elvet Moorman, who claimed to have seen Holmes and the little boy and helped to move a large "Peninsular Oak" wood burning stove onto the property.

Some newspaper accounts recount that the stove was removed from the cottage and shipped to Philadelphia

The Mystery of the H. H. Holmes Collection

for the trial IN 1895. Therefore, it must also be assumed that Geyer gathered all of the remaining evidence: the doomed boy's remains, burnt photos, bits of clothing and other evidence gathered at the Irvington crime scene to be used at the trial in Philadelphia. Since Holmes was never tried for the murder of young Howard, the evidence disappeared.

There is a cabinet card in the collection that resembles the distinctive looking Geyer. The image was taken at the Miner & Dexter photography studio at 44 Calhoun Street in Fort Wayne, Indiana. Charles Winslow Miner (1866–1912) was a prominent photographer in that city from 1887 through the early 1900s. He is best known for his studio portraits and commercial photographs of land-

Detective Geyer.

Contemporary courtroom sketch of Detective Geyer.

Cabinet card from the Holmes Collection.

The Mystery of the H. H. Holmes Collection

marks in Allen County, Indiana, especially the Allen County Courthouse and notable Fort Wayne businesses. His photographs were published in Fort Wayne booster books in the early 1900s. Miner became nationally known for his portraits, photo enlargements, and "color work." In the July 13, 1910 issue of The *Fort Wayne Sentinel*, the name of Frank Geyer appears in conjunction with The Eagles annual picnic at Central Park on the 21st of August. Geyer's name also appears in the December 28, 1891 and December 30, 1916 issues of the *Sentinel* newspaper.

Miner suffered a severe asthma attack in November 1911 and died six months later at the young age of 45. Miner later at his home in Fort Wayne. The Indiana Historical Society re-created the interior of Miner's Studio, ca. 1904, as part of its "You Are There" exhibitions at the Eugene and Marilyn Glick Indiana History Center in Indianapolis and hold many of his images.

Frank Geyer died at the age of 64 from heart disease on October 4, 1918. Hundreds of policeman and detectives attended his funeral. He is buried in Hillside cemetery in Roslyn, Pennsylvania.

Absent the work of Detective Geyer, it is quite likely that H.H. Holmes would have served only a short jail term for insurance fraud. Without Geyer, Holmes' killing would have been only briefly interrupted. Could the Holmes Collection have once been the property of Detective Frank Geyer? Was the Irvington evidence deemed irrelevant after Holmes's conviction for the murder of Ben Pitezel, and yet it was keep as a reminder of a highpoint in his career?

While we may never know the answer to these

The Mystery of the H. H. Holmes Collection

questions, it does seem likely that if Geyer himself assembled this macabre collection, he may have found it difficult to simply dispose of them. Geyer was a thorough man and a seasoned investigator and when it came to the slippery Dr. Holmes, well, you just never knew.

The Mystery of the H. H. Holmes Collection

Herman Webster Mudgett, *aka* Dr. H. H. Holmes

At this point, we've explored the possibility of ownership by investigating several likely subjects. But are we missing the most obvious culprit?

Could the objects in the Holmes archive collection have belonged to H.H. Holmes himself?

The idea of H.H. Holmes as a collector is not hard to understand. He has proven his apparent need to acquire souvenirs time and time again. But why? What drove him to save this "stuff"? His intent may have been an insatiable desire to demonstrate dominance over his victims, or to relive his crimes, or to commemorate the deceased.

Herman Webster Mudgett, aka Dr. H. H. Holmes.

In my opinion, H.H. Holmes viewed these relics, some of which held meaning only to him, as the supreme form of trophy-taking. For a narcissistic psychopath like Holmes, taking souvenirs offered an opportunity to play

The Mystery of the H. H. Holmes Collection

God by his own warped form of reclamation.

An article titled "The Master of the Murder Castle" appeared in the December 1943 issue of **Harper's Magazine**. In it H.H. Holmes was described this way:

"He deserves to rank with the great criminals of history. Crime writers reserve the word "monster" for top-notch murderers. A monster ranks above such lesser criminals as fiends, beasts, and phantoms. He must meet certain rigid requirements. His victims, killed over a period of years and not for money alone, must be numerous and preferably female, and he must do unusual things with their bodies; he must inhabit a gloomy, forbidding dwelling, and he should be of a scientific bent. The master of the murder castle possessed all these qualifications and more. Magnificent swindler, petty cheat, mass murderer, he was a man of nimble, tortuous mind. He pyramided fraud upon fraud. Young, good-looking, glib, he mesmerized business men and captivated and seduced pretty young women, at least two of whom he married bigamously. Physician, student of hypnotism, dabbler in the occult, gentleman of fashion, devious liar, skillful manipulator of amazingly complex enterprises, he died on the gallows when he was thirty-five, his crimes exposed accidentally by the vengeful suspicions of that most despised figure in crime, the police informer."

After all, the Holmes archive collection fits quite well with what we know about Holmes and his many personality traits. In Holmes' day, the photograph was a common symbol of friendship and admiration. They were the utmost symbol of esteem during the Victorian Era. Although it may be hard to fathom in today's social media selfie driven society, in Holmes' day a person may have only had their picture taken a few times in their life. If someone honored you with their photograph, you were special.

The Mystery of the H. H. Holmes Collection

Given Holmes' reputation as a womanizer, photos would be the perfect souvenir. That same 1943 **Harper's Magazine** article commented on Holmes penchant for photographs:

"All his girls were pretty and many were his stenographers. His favorites he had photographed "in the pose and dress affected by actresses." He once displayed these photographs to an acquaintance in his apartments, perhaps while the girls' bodies were decomposing in the cellar below."

Holmes was the consummate con man, an unapologetic thief and admitted serial killer. Photos and personal objects could easily be used in insurance scams and other assorted cons. Assuming that many of these objects were stolen from his victims, the simple act of taking them surely fueled the thief in H.H. Holmes. Holmes the murderer would most certainly have delighted at the thought of looking at this collection as a macabre walk down memory lane.

Despite the fact that Holmes was a known con man and suspected murderer, his neighbors in multiple towns said that he was handsome, charming, and charismatic to the extreme. He could sweet talk his way in and out of almost any situation. Holmes neighbors also said that he was generous, frequently giving out gifts and lending people money. Of course, the money and the items were stolen, and some people knew that, but they all commented on how readily Holmes was willing to share his stolen possessions and money. When Holmes was arrested for murder, many of his neighbors refused to believe that he could be a murderer. Most believed he was a pretty good guy, who was a little odd.

If indeed this collection belonged to H.H. Holmes, it offers another glimpse into the hubris of the man himself. Perhaps

The Mystery of the H. H. Holmes Collection

Holmes felt himself invincible, we already know he considered himself to be above the law. Holmes probably never considered that these souvenirs could be his undoing by providing physical evidence linking him to his victims while providing a crushing blow to his defense case in the courtroom. Holmes desire to steal and keep souvenirs could be irrefutable proof that pursuing police had the right man.

While the motivations and methods of murder for H.H. Holmes may have differed, his desire to keep mementos (such as the unposted letters from the Pitezel children) inevitably sealed his fate. The sense of pleasure Holmes obtained from these items kept his murderous acts alive in his mind and even when caught and imprisoned for his crimes, the memories remained. Perhaps, alone in his Moyamensing prison cell, the absence of these souvenirs contributed to Holmes descent into madness and personal conviction that he had become the devil himself.

Part Four

Epilogue

The Mystery of the H. H. Holmes Collection

Hoosier Ties & Anomalies.

Lineville, Indiana

The crimes of H.H. Holmes have a way of popping up generations after America's first serial killer was hanged in Philadelphia.

In 1919, a discovery in Lake County, Indiana, brought Holmes back into the news. In court twenty-four years earlier, Holmes had mentioned killing two people near Schneider, a tiny town on the outskirts of the old Kankakee Marsh in southern Lake County. According to the pewspapers of the time, this remote spot, known as Lineville, is located roughly twelve miles east of Momence, Illinois and forty miles south of Gary, almost straddling the Indiana-Illinois state line.

Today, Lineville is an obscure ghost town, not found on any map. It disappeared more than a century ago. Lineville was a tiny railroad station or switch right on the state line. This was probably the kind of place where trains took on duck meat and frog legs hunted in the swamp and served for breakfast in the dining cars.

Although the disappearance of Lineville is inter-

The Mystery of the H. H. Holmes Collection

esting, the identity of Holmes' alleged victims is a more intriguing mystery. In October 1919, two skeletons were discovered on Ira G. Mansfield's farm. An October 22 article in Hammond's **Lake County Times** brought back those dark Gilded Age memories from the south side of Chicago.

> "New Victims of H.H. Holmes Found Near Lowell...A man by the name of Davis of Momence says that he remembers a man and a woman came to Momence with Holmes and together they went to the Three-I depot and bought tickets for Lineville and later Holmes was seen in Momence, but nothing further was seen or heard of the man and woman who was with him. Where the bones were found there was no trace of a casket and that together with the bullet holes in one of the skulls would indicate that the two people were murdered and buried there under the old log cabin. The bodies were found buried about 6 feet apart and may have been placed there at different times. Every indication is that Holmes murdered them and placed them there. Another witness, Mr. Alexander Black, declares that he well remembers the day that Holmes and the woman came to Momence. They were at the hotel and the woman had been crying."

The Father Patrick J. Dailey Bible

Another interesting souvenir recently surfaced in Philadelphia, found tucked away in a Bible. A New Jersey couple, Claire and Larry Fanelle, were cleaning out Claire's mother's old books when she stumbled upon a

The Mystery of the H. H. Holmes Collection

Bible, it's covers missing, pages loose and dog-eared. Like many a family Bible, there were newspaper clippings and handwritten notes and mementos hidden between many of the pages inside. As Fanelle's son perused the newspaper clippings, Claire came across a ragged edged handwritten note.

The note was signed by a name that had been peppering the local news lately. She remembered hearing that the TV program, **The American Ripper**, was exhuming the body this controversial man from the nearby Yeadon cemetery near Philadelphia for a DNA test. The note that she held in her hands bore the distinctive signature of H.H. Holmes.

The Bible she found belonged to the first cousin of her great grandfather, Father Patrick J. Dailey, a Catholic priest once stationed at the Annunciation of the Blessed Virgin Mary, which is very near the prison Holmes was kept in. Fanelle family tradition states that Father Dailey ministered to inmates awaiting execution, including Holmes. The family believes the note, written on May 7, 1896, the day of Holmes' execution, was probably handed to Father Dailey on the way to the gallows.

The letter reads,

"Dear Father Dailey, I must write and make you know the kind feelings I have for you, but fear I can't. I know that you by God's Grace have done much to save my soul from eternal damnation. I need your prayers after my death. With all of my heart – H.H. Holmes, May 7. 1896."

The Fanelle's were surprised to find the note and felt that if nothing else, it proved that Holmes felt remorse for his

The Mystery of the H. H. Holmes Collection

crimes and may have tried to turn his life around during his final days. Holmes researchers disagree and say the note is typical self-serving rhetoric from a man desperate to save his skin. In 21st century vernacular, Holmes was determined to "Never drop the con, die with the lie."

A Souvenier [sic] from "Holmes Castle."

In the January 1898 issue of ***The Ologist***, a monthly magazine for "the student of birds, their nests and eggs". This issue carries a classified ad reads:

> *"A Souvenier [sic] from "Holmes Castle." Send ten cents for a package of Asbestos (mineral wood) which was taken from around the dummy safe in which H.H. Holmes suffocated many of his victims. Holmes was executsd [sic] in Philadelphia on the charge of killing Pretzel [sic], his partner in crime. Twenty-three murders have been charged two [sic] Holmes.*
>
> > *Clifton A. Fox*
> > *525 W. 61st St.*
> > *Chicago Ill."*

It is interesting to note that Mr. Fox lived on 61st Street and the Murder Castle was located at 63rd and Wallace.

Final Thoughts

Yes indeed, America's first serial killer came through Irvington. He walked the streets, plotted his crime and planned his escape from what was once the far eastern side of old Irvington. Why Irvington? Why did he come here? Most importantly, why was it the last place that Detective Frank Geyer searched on the eve of his final departure for Chicago? Because Irvington was home to Butler College. The best, the brightest, the cream of Indianapolis society lived here and surely, Holmes would never hide out here. He wouldn't dare, would he? Yes, he would and yes he did.

Although undeniably detestable, H. H. Holmes remains a irresistible, enigmatic character in American history. His time in Indianapolis, let alone in Irvington, is barely mentioned in most biographies, but his visit to the Hoosier Capitol left a mark that may just recently have resurfaced.

The search for Howard was complete, Holmes was convicted, executed and buried, The curse of H.H. Holmes continues to be discussed and the mystery of the H.H.

The Mystery of the H. H. Holmes Collection

Holmes Collection continues.

Who created this singular collection? Did Holmes keep it as mementos of his crimes? Did his friend from the university, Charles W. Miller collect it? Or his partner in crime and victim, Benjamin Pitezel, or maybe his handyman, Pat Quinlan? Maybe it belonged to his surviving wife, Georgiana Yoke? Or his secretary, Emeline Cigrand? Or one of the Detectives, David Richards or Frank Geyer? Or….?

The truth is, we just don't know who complied this collection, or why it was created.

More importantly, we do not know the many faces found in this collection. Are they simply a collection of friends and relatives, or are they the only traces left of the hundreds of men, women and children that H.H. Holmes might have murdered.

If you can help us identify any of the unknown faces in this collection, we hope that you will contact us at *BonaHolmesMystery@gmail.com*.

Alan E. Hunter
September 2017

Further Reading

Borowski, John. *The Strange Case Of Dr. H.H. Holmes.* 2008 Waterfront Productions ISBN-13: 9780975918517

Geyer, Frank P. *The Holmes – Pitezel case. A history of the greatest crime of the century and the search for the missing Pitezel children.* London : Forgotten Books, 2015.

Larsen, Eric. *The Devil in the White City.* New York : Crown Publishers, c2003.

Nickels, Judith. *A Competent Witness: Georgiana Yoke and the Trial of H. H. Holmes.* North Charleston, SC : CreateSpace Independent Publishing Platform, 2014. ISBN 13: 9781497381926.

Schechter, Harold. *Depraved: The Definitive True Story of H.H. Holmes, Whose Grotesque Crimes Shattered Turn-of-the-Century Chicago.* New York : Pocket Books, 1994.

Hoosier State Chronicles. This collection provides free, online access to high quality digital images of historic Indiana newspapers published between 1804 and 2010. https://newspapers.library.in.gov/

Other Titles of Interest

Hunter, Alan E and Joseph M. Jarzen. *Indiana's Historic National Road: The East Side from Richmond to Indianapolis*. (Images of America). 2011 : Arcadia Publishing. ISBN 13: 9780738560557.

Hunter, Alan E and Joseph M. Jarzen. *Indiana's Historic National Road: The West Side from Richmond to Indianapolis* (Images of America). 2011 : Arcadia Publishing. ISBN 13: 9780738560557.

Hunter, Alan E and Russ Simnick. *Irvington Haunts.* Haunted History Publishing. ISBN 0976095203.

Hunter, Alan E and Russ Simnick. *More Irvington Haunts*. 2008 Haunted History Publishing. ISBN 9780976095217.

Hunter, Alan E. *Bumps in the Night. Stories from the Weekly View*. 2014 : Haunted History Publishing. ISBN 9781467545068.

Hunter, Alan E. *Indianapolis Haunts*. 2012 : Haunted History Publishing. ISBN 9781467545051.

Hunter, Alan E. *Irvington Haunts. The Tour Guide*. 2015 : Haunted History Publishing. ISBN 9781467545075.

ABOUT THE AUTHOR

Alan E. Hunter has researched, scripted and lead the Irvington Ghost Walks for over 15 years. The tours are roughly 75% history and 25 % ghost stories and folklore. These non-profit tours raise much needed funds for the Eastside Irvington community. In addition, Al has led similar tours in Greenfield and Cambridge City on the Historic National Road. As a former Vice-President and board member of the Indiana National Road Association and is active in Irvington Historic Society.

He has co-authored two books on haunted Irvington and two books on the Historic Indiana National Road. In 2013, Al published a compilation of his "Bumps in the Night" articles, a weekly column he writes for the *Weekly View* newspaper. Over the past few years, Al has led talks and programs in Irvington that have collected food and personal care items for the Irvington homeless shelter, gathering well over a ton of food, clothing and personal care goods for distribution.

A former teacher and baseball coach at Westfield High School, Al graduated from Indiana University and has been married to his wife Rhonda for nearly 30 years. They have 2 children, daughter Jasmine and son Addison and 2 dogs, Spartacus (Sparky) and Ace (Acey).

The Mystery of the H. H. Holmes Collection